"In a recent study on the effectiveness of Catholic Religious Education/Catechesis, two qualities of adult Catholics were mentioned: 1) committed to the proclamation of the gospel, and 2) reads/reflects on scripture. *The Word of the Lord* speaks directly to these qualities. As a popular commentary this book flows out of the experience that McBrien has had with many different ministers of the Word and will assist adult Catholics and those who minister to them in their lifelong formation as disciples of Jesus."

Matthew J. Hayes
Executive Director
Office of Formation & Education
Louisville, Kentucky

"*The Word of the Lord: Reflections on the Sunday Readings* by Philip McBrien is a 'popular' lectionary commentary that offers a particular perspective on the weekly readings, raising interesting and important issues for the reader through summaries of the readings and reflective questions. This book may be useful in providing insight to lectors, guidance to discussion leaders of small faith-sharing or catechumenate groups, and as a resource for individuals seeking a simple introductory understanding of the biblical text."

Tricia Boyle
Faith Education Coordinator
Queen of Peace Catholic Church
Salem, Oregon

"This easy-to-use primer on the Sunday lections is a welcome resource for busy pastoral ministers who are ever alert for quality materials for various groups. It provides:

- A handy supplement to existing parish Bible study groups, especially in light of the well-crafted questions for reflection.
- An enticing sampler for parishioners who exhibit a beginning curiosity about the study of Scripture.
- A useful tool for thoughtful lectors as they prepare, individually or communally, to proclaim the Word in the assembly.
- A ready companion for individuals who have already incorporated *Lectio Divina* into their way of prayer.
- A well-constructed resource for ecumenical or convenanted communities who utilize the Common Lectionary for faith sharing."

Gretchen Hailer, RSHM
Consultant, Faith Formation

"I recommend *The Word of the Lord* to lectors, preachers, liturgy planners, Scripture study groups, Renew groups, and catechumens. The commentary on each reading is concise but packed with insights from the most current scriptural studies. Following each Sunday's commentaries are probing 'questions for reflection.' These take readers from the page to their own lived experience of church, nudging them toward an appreciation of the Scripture readings, both personally and communally."

Father George J. Wolf, Pastor
Queen of Peace Catholic Church
Salem, Oregon

# The

# *Word*

## of the Lord

### Reflections on the Sunday Readings

### YEAR A

## PHILIP J. MCBRIEN

XXIII

TWENTY-THIRD PUBLICATIONS

Mystic, CT 06355

Twenty-Third Publications
185 Willow Street
P.O. Box 180
Mystic, CT 06355
(203) 536-2611
800-321-0411

ISBN 0-89622-659-X
Library of Congress Catalog Card Number 95-60665
Printed in the U.S.A.

For Patrick and Brendan

# Acknowledgments

This book is a fruit of a conversation that has gone on for many years and that has included many people. Through a few weeks of intense activity, I have harvested the fruit and done some of the preparation necessary to present it to you. Had it not been for the wise voices of many others, however, this would have been a very different and lesser work.

I owe much to the people and pastoral staff of St. Thomas Aquinas parish in Indianapolis, with whom I participated in serious conversations with the lectionary for many years. I thank especially Julie Niec, Fr. Cliff Vogelsang, Patti Hair, Betty Bopp, Tom Agnew, Bill Bensch, Mary Henehan Yarger, Mary Carson and Norma Carrigan. It was my privilege to work with these good people on various projects related to the lectionary. In his or her own way, whether in insight or in correcting my crazy notions, each has helped to shape the book you hold in your hands. Dr. Ron Allen of Christian Theological Seminary also lent his eloquent voice to the conversation, and introduced me to many others as well.

More recently, Dan Connors, Jennifer Johnson, and Neil Kluepfel have polished the fruit and made it possible to offer it to you. And most of all I am indebted to my wife, the Rev. Dana Morgan McBrien, whose occasionally nettlesome but always intelligent questions remind me that conversation is as important for life as the air we breathe.

# Contents

# INTRODUCTION

On the fifteenth Sunday in ordinary time we read verses from one of the greatest of all poems:

> For as the rain and the snow come down from the sky
> and do not return there but water the earth,
> making it bring forth and sprout,
> giving seed to one who sows and bread to one who eats
> so shall my word be that goes forth from my mouth;
> it shall not return to me empty,
> but it shall accomplish that which I intend,
> and prosper in the thing for which I sent it.
> —Isaiah 55:10–11

God's word falls upon the earth and immediately goes to work. As water carves mountains and valleys, God's word gives shape to the world around us. As water causes much of the earth to bloom with vegetation and the land and the seas to teem with creatures, God's word gives life. As water provides seed for sowing and bread for eating, God's word feeds us and keeps us alive. Most of all, God sends both water and word to cause health, happiness, and justice among people.

Since before time began, the word of the Lord has permeated our earth and our lives. God's word is too big and too powerful to be encompassed in the pages of a book, or for that matter, in the pages of all the books that could ever be written. Even the Bible cannot contain *all* of God's word. Why, then, do I dare to call this book *The Word of the Lord?*

I conceive it as a keyhole through which you can look upon the larger reality it hopes to introduce to you. The subtitle describes the book's focus: It invites you to hear God's word through *reflections on the Sunday readings* used by the Roman Catholic Church.

Above all this book is an invitation to you. It tells you one author's ideas about the contents of some important parts of God's word. If I have done my job, the book invites you to go beyond my reflections to listen more deeply to God's word in prayer and action, in continued Scripture study, and in the people and the world around you.

## How to Use This Book

To understand the scheme of the book, you must know something about the Sunday readings. Catholic worship is guided by prayers and rituals, and by biblical texts arranged into a schedule, or calendar. The prayers and rituals have been bound into a book we call the sacramentary. We call our arrangement of biblical texts the lectionary. (Together, these two parts comprise the *Roman Missal*, the sourcebook for Mass.) The lectionary assigns readings to each day of every week in every year. Sundays and principal feasts make up a fraction of the lectionary. Moreover, the lectionary is constructed upon not one, but two cycles, or calendars. The more familiar calendar is known as the "temporal cycle." It schedules the various seasons of the year and the feasts that define those seasons. Sundays and the principal feast days are assigned readings according to a three-year rotation. Each year in the rotation is designated A, B, or C. Weekdays are assigned readings according to a two-year cycle.

The less familiar calendar is known as the "sanctoral cycle." As its name suggests, this is primarily a cycle of saints' feast days, but it also includes solemnities such as the Transfiguration (August 6), the Holy Cross (September 14), and others. These feasts displace weekday readings whenever they occur, and once in a while they displace Sunday readings. In 2008, for example, the thirteenth Sunday in ordinary time will be displaced by the solemnity of Saints Peter and Paul, Apostles, which is always celebrated on June 29.

This book deals with the readings of year A Sundays and feast days according to the temporal cycle, and with only those other feasts that we know as "holy days of obligation." Otherwise it omits the sanctoral cycle.

There are, therefore, some sixty-eight chapters in the book. Each is identified by the Sunday or solemnity whose readings it considers, and each contains the following:

•A theme that I have found among the readings. Keep in mind that it is one of many possible themes, and that if you study the texts in detail, you might find entirely different themes, or even none at all. I include mine to focus the reflections.

•Dates, in brackets. Here is an example: Since 1995-96 is year A in Catholic reckoning, that year's readings for the first Sunday in Advent are to be used on December 3, 1995. Now although Advent happens every year, the following year will be year B and the next, year C. On the First Sunday of Advent in those years the church uses different sets of readings. The year A readings for the first Sunday of Advent will be in effect on November 29, 1998, and again on December 2, 2001, and every third year following. Each chapter names the next three dates upon which its readings are to be used.

•Complete references for, quotations from, and reflections on the day's first reading, second reading, and gospel. Only a reference is provided for the day's responsorial psalm, because unlike the other texts which may be poetry, history, story, or other literary form, a psalm is always a prayer. Preferring not to comment on the psalms, instead I invite you to pray them. Read them (or even better sing them) aloud, and savor their beauty.

•Questions. I intend these to be challenging. They ask for your careful consideration and for action. They clarify the various challenges borne in the texts they accompany. You will not answer them completely, on first, second, or even third encounter. I hope they spark your thinking and action, both now and in years to come.

## What This Book Can Do

Now that you know how the book is structured, allow me to tell you what it can do:

•*Summarize readings and offer a particular perspective on them.* I assume that your experience of hearing readings proclaimed and explained at Mass leaves you hungry for more. You do not wish to commit to hard, technical Scripture study, but you are willing to invest a little time and energy to acquaint yourself with the readings in use at Mass. You seek simple explanations of these texts.

•*Provoke your reflection on issues raised by the readings.* The Bible is arguably the most influential collection of literature ever produced. Its many and varied texts bear the power to change lives. When we devote even a casual attention to biblical texts, as we are doing here, inevitably we raise important, sometimes vital issues. This book directs your attention to some of those issues, especially with the questions that accompany each Sunday's or solemnity's set of readings.

•*Help you to prepare to proclaim texts publicly.* If you are a lector or a teacher, or if you read aloud at any form of prayer service, you need at least a simple understanding of your text. Your job is not to analyze a text or to guide people into its intricacies. Homilists, exegetes, and other specialists do those things. Still, you must present your text clearly and with confidence. After all, your text is an important part of God's word. If you can know a little about what a text says, you have taken the first step toward proclaiming it with confidence. If you have not the slightest notion of what is going on in a text, on the other hand, you cannot proclaim it well. Since some biblical texts are, quite frankly, difficult, maybe you can use a simple guide.

•*Focus a small group of Christian friends in discussion.* Since our origins, we Christians have been a talkative bunch. The first impulse of people who meet the risen Christ has always been to run out and announce the good news to someone else. Even those witnesses portrayed at the end of Mark's gospel, ordered not to say anything, must have disobeyed and blabbed. Had they not, and had no one else told the story, there might be no Christian books in the Bible.

One way we encounter the risen Christ is by reading the Bible, even when texts do not speak of the resurrection. We can talk about what we find there. Like those blabby witnesses in Mark's gospel, we *must* talk about it. This book can provide a focus for your deep conversations with spouses and friends, and for faith-sharing group meetings.

•*Provide a simple guidebook for your parish catechumenate,* or for any interreligious gathering of friends wishing to sample the lectionary's riches. Although my primary audience is Christian, particularly Roman Catholic, there is no reason to exclude anyone from your conversations and faith sharing. I have used many of the questions listed in this book with groups that included Jews, Muslims, Buddhists, agnostics, and atheists. The human issues raised in biblical texts are universal. Anyone who wishes to converse about them can and should be welcomed into conversation. Keep in mind that a genuine welcome never downplays our Christian identity. It does, however, require that we listen sensitively and respectfully to other voices.

Keeping all these things in mind, you may find that this book works well as a discussion guide in your parish catechumenate. This is true because the lectionary does seem to have been arranged, in part, to invite all persons into continuing conversion. When catechumens are dismissed from liturgy to pray, to share faith, and to explore the readings, their catechists may find the questions presented here useful.

•*Provide a simple sourcebook for spiritual directors and the people they direct.* The lectionary's texts and the questions in the book invite reflection and action. They invite you to examine your choices clearly, and to enact those choices that are most compatible with the good news of Jesus. But this is precisely the invitation of most forms of spiritual direction.

•*Serve as a supplement for family religious education.* The lectionary has found ever wider use in religious education in recent years, though not without some controversy. One advantage claimed by proponents is that since all generations hear the same readings proclaimed at worship, it is a simple matter to focus inter-generation education programs on these texts. While children are not likely to read this book, it can help parents to explain the Sunday and feast day readings to their children. This book can help your family to read, discuss, and pray with the Sunday readings.

•*Invite you to read, study, and interpret biblical texts.* The book is an introduction. Consider it a taste, a sampler, even a teaser. Most of all, it wants to invite you to immerse yourself in history's most important collection of words. I hope you will hear this invitation.

## What This Book Will Not Do

Having told you what my book can do, I must make some disclaimers. It will not:

•*Take the place of your direct encounter with biblical texts.* Nothing should ever be allowed to stand in the way of your encounter with the magnificent literature in our Bible. It would be a cruel irony if a book called *The Word of the Lord* prevented you from hearing or even trying to hear the word of the Lord. If you must choose between one or the other, drop this book immediately, and read your Bible or lectionary. After you have wrestled with the real thing, come back to my book, if you wish. Parts of the Bible will edify you and challenge you. Other parts are sure to confuse you or even infuriate you. Maybe I can help you begin to sort some things out.

•*Provide you with the definitive interpretation of any biblical text, or pretend to make any such interpretation.* This book will not tell you what a text means, although I have made every effort to help you to see what each text says. There is a difference. Throughout this book I want to help you make sense of each text on a most simple level. It takes hard work to interpret texts responsibly (see Appendix), but I presume that you are reading this book because you have not yet decided to do hard interpretive work. I have done some of the necessary hard work to set a simple explanation of readings before you.

But isn't any statement of what a text says a form of interpretation? Isn't it a statement of what the text means? After all, we humans are meaning-making creatures. Constantly, relentlessly, we try to figure things out, to determine what things mean. Moreover, we interpret in ways shaped by our unique funds of experience.

Yes, when I describe for you what I see happening in a text, I give it a particular slant, an interpretation. This is unavoidable, and I will not pretend otherwise. But my point here concerns not what I have written but the manner in which I invite you to read it. Please read it as introduction only, and not as the last word, not as *the* meaning of any text.

• *Equip you with specialized tools for interpretation. The Word of the Lord* is a form of biblical commentary, more properly a lectionary commentary. But all commentaries are not alike, nor are all created equal.

A peek into any decent bookstore shows you shelf upon shelf of commentaries on the Bible. Lectionary commentaries are likely to appear only in catalogs and specialized bookstores, but they are also quite numerous. Why are there so many? The quick answer is to say that the various commentaries address differing audiences, for specific purposes.

To understand this latter point more clearly, it helps to think of the various commentaries under two broad headings. "Scholarly" commentaries tend to be detailed, technical, usually intimidating, and often hard to read. That's the bad news. The good news is that the best scholarly works help us to open up texts, sometimes to find things we would almost certainly never see without their help. They equip us to dive deep into the waters of Scripture and to stay underwater for serious expeditions.

"Popular" commentaries, by contrast, tend to speak in general, non-technical terms. They try to be accessible and easy to read. Unlike scholarly works, however, they tend to close texts, rather than to open them. They help us to see only what can be seen fairly easily. They help us to stay afloat on the surface of the Bible, but they cannot sustain us under the surface for more than a few moments.

All of this is not to say that one kind of commentary is better than another. As I said earlier, there are differing audiences with specific needs and interests. It is legitimate that different kinds of commentaries address differing audiences.

This distinction will help you to understand what you can expect from this book. It is a "popular" commentary, in the technical sense in which I have used that word. I have used many of the best available scholarly works to produce it, and it is as reliable as I can make it, but it is not a work of scholarship. Many times I will tell you that "scholars say this" and "scholars say that." A scholarly work would try to demonstrate why scholars say what they say about any given text. Here I report on the fruits of scholarship, in order to offer a simple explanation of what each text says. To go deeper, you must use a scholarly commentary, ideally in a form of conversation (see Appendix).

•*Guide you through the mechanics of lector preparation.* I said earlier that a basic understanding of a text is your first step toward proclaiming it well. It is not the only step, however. *The Word of the Lord* equips you with an understanding of each text. It does not teach you about posture, elocution, tone, pace, or any of the other ingredients of excellent proclamation. Some books do try to assist you in these ways, but I think your better option is a sensitive coach. All the better if he or she is equipped with a video camera.

### Listen for the Word

The prophet has insisted that God's word is all around us and in us. God's word saturates the earth, seeking every opportunity to fulfill the purpose for which God has spoken. This volume of *The Word of the Lord* invites you beyond its own modest efforts to listen for God's word, in the Scriptures, in your choices and actions, and in the world. Forthcoming volumes will provide reflections on Sunday and holy day readings for years B and C. For now I hope you enjoy my efforts with the year A readings.

# FIRST SUNDAY OF ADVENT

*Make peace, not war*

[December 3, 1995; November 29, 1998; December 2, 2001]

### First Reading: Isaiah 2:1–5

*They shall beat their swords into plowshares.*

Advent always begins with a prophetic summons inviting us to imagine a world restored to health, a world of divine promises fulfilled. At the beginning of year A, Isaiah asks us to picture the mountain of the Lord's house established above all other peaks, and all the nations of the earth streaming to it and gathering at its base. Instruction and judgment will be given at the mountain. In response, the people will beat their swords into plowshares and their spears into pruning hooks. There will be no more wars, nor training for war. Instruments of death will be reshaped into tools that sustain life.

The reading concludes with a direct invitation to the prophet's original audience: "Come, house of Jacob, and walk in the light of the Lord." Christians have always taken this invitation as their own as well. Behind the images we hear a simple invitation to make peace and walk in the light of the Lord.

Can there be a more appropriate way to begin a new year?

### Responsorial Psalm:
### Psalm 122:1–2, 3–4, 4–5, 6–7, 8–9

### Second Reading: Romans 13:11–14

*Let us cast off deeds of darkness....*
*Let us live honorably as in daylight.*

Some scholars insist that Paul expected the end of the world to occur within his lifetime, and that this expectation fed the urgency we see in today's reading and in others like it. In these verses the mutually reinforcing images of sleep and darkness insist that the night is nearly over, that we must awake from our sleep. We must stop doing things that we used to hide under the cover of darkness. We must now start to live honorably, as though it is daylight and all of our actions and desires are in plain view. We must leave behind all of our sinful habits. Paul urges us to wear the Lord Jesus Christ like a suit of clothes, and therefore to give up any concerns for what Paul calls the "desires of the flesh." Our new attire will give us everything we need.

## Gospel: Matthew 24:37–44

*Stay awake...! You cannot know the day your Lord is coming.*

Here is one of Jesus' most frightening teachings. He reminds the disciples of the time of Noah, when people ignored invitations to change, right up until the flood destroyed them. Similarly, when the Son of Man comes a catastrophe will befall the world. Some people will be taken up into safety, while others will be left behind, presumably to be destroyed. The final three verses shed light on this teaching. If you knew the precise time when a thief was coming to rob you, you would prepare yourself in every possible way to protect your household. No one knows when the Son of Man will come, so the prudent thing is to stay awake now, to make yourself ready now.

Advent is about urgency. Wake up! Prepare for the arrival of the one who is to come. There is no time to lose. Make peace now, because he comes like a thief.

## Questions for Reflection

•We are constantly making choices. How often do you choose to act in violent, warlike ways? How often do you act peacefully? How can you start to make peaceful choices? What are the swords that you can beat into tools that give life and peace?

•What are the deeds of darkness that go on in your neighborhood, your parish, your town? What deeds of darkness continue to plague our world? How do you continue to act as though it were still night, as though Christ had not yet turned the night into day?

•How can you prepare yourself for the one who comes like a thief? What will you do to get ready?

# SECOND SUNDAY OF ADVENT
## The reign of God is at hand
[December 10, 1995; December 6, 1998; December 9, 2001]

### First Reading: Isaiah 11:1–10
*On that day...there shall be no harm or ruin on all my holy mountain;*
*for the earth shall be filled with knowledge of the Lord.*

We are treated to a feast of images. The first reminds us of David. A shoot shall sprout from the stump of Jesse, and the spirit of God shall rest upon him. He will not judge by appearance. Instead, he shall wear the divine attributes of justice and faithfulness around his waist. On that day the wolf will be guest of the lamb, and the leopard shall nestle with the kid. The calf and the lion will play together, led by a little child. Prey and predator will embrace in peace, because the earth will be filled with knowledge of the Lord.

For Christians, the shoot from Jesse is the *Messiah*, the anointed one, the *Christ*. The Messiah has come. Eventually he will transform the world so that all natural enemies may play together. Someday, the baby will even play by the cobra's den. On that day every last nook and cranny in creation will be filled with knowledge of God, as water covers everything in the sea.

### Responsorial Psalm: Psalm 72:1–2, 7–8, 12–13, 17

### Second Reading: Romans 15:4–9
*Accept one another...as Christ accepted you, for the glory of God.*

The only Scriptures known to Paul are what we sometimes call the "old testament." Writing to Christians who seem to have had no understanding of things Jewish and who may have wanted to discard them, Paul insists that the Scriptures encourage and teach all. He also prays that God will enable his audience to live in perfect harmony.

If we take this message to heart, we must accept one another in the same manner as Christ has accepted us, for the glory of God. We must understand that Christ became the servant of the Jews because God has always remained faithful to promises given to the patriarchs. Paul echoes Isaiah's invitation to the Gentiles, and to us: "Come to the Lord's mountain."

## Gospel: Matthew 3:1–12

*Reform your lives! The reign of God is at hand.*

Since ancient times, the church has used the second Sunday of Advent to direct our attention to John the Baptizer. An itinerant preacher whose appearance and diet reminded people of the great prophet Elijah, John drew people from Jerusalem, Judea, and all the surrounding region to hear him preach and to be baptized. The core of his message was, "Reform your lives, repent of your sins. The reign of God is at hand."

In this scene from Matthew's gospel some of the recognized religious leaders of the day step forward for their baptisms, and John accosts them. He insists that it is not enough to be a descendant of Abraham, for God can raise up children of Abraham from stones lying on the ground. Introducing the image of a tree, he tells his audience, and us, to bear fruit or to be felled and thrown into the fire.

This glimpse at first-century Jewish baptism tells us that the motives that propel our actions are far more important than the actions themselves. To enter into the ritual bath of purification, we must confess our sins, reform our lives, and begin to live as though the reign of God were here. We, too, must take on the challenge of preparing the way for the Lord.

## Questions for Reflection

•How often do you make judgments on the basis of appearance or hearsay? How do you think the Messiah's way of justice differs from the way in which you habitually conduct yourself?

•Whom do you find hard to accept? What does today's second reading insist that you do?

•What kinds of privileges do your station in life, education, profession, ethnic background, financial status, and religion lead you to expect? What does today's gospel text seem to say to your expectations? How does it challenge you?

•What has your baptism cost you? How has your baptism placed obligations upon you? How well do you live up to your obligations? What changes must you make?

# THIRD SUNDAY OF ADVENT

*The one who is to come*

[December 17, 1995; December 13, 1998; December 16, 2001]

### First Reading: Isaiah 35:1–6, 10

*They will meet with joy and gladness, sorrow and mourning will flee.*

The eighth-century prophet Isaiah advised kings during turbulent years in the ancient kingdom of Judah. The first forty chapters of the book bearing his name present visions, political analyses, and, occasionally, powerful images describing God's eternal faithfulness. Today's reading offers images of promise. "The desert shall bear fruit, and God will be revealed to the nations. All who are weak or infirm must take heart, for your God comes to save you, to establish justice, to ransom all who have suffered."

God's promise is both particular and universal. Recognizing the historical sufferings and captivities of the chosen people, Isaiah offers assurance that God will bring them back to Jerusalem in triumph. These verses also seem to promise to all people a time of singing, of celebrating, a time in which sorrow and mourning will flee from the world.

### Responsorial Psalm: Psalm 146:6–7, 8–9, 9–10

### Second Reading: James 5:7–10

*See how the farmer awaits the precious yield of the soil....*
*You too, must be patient.*

James invites Christians to await the Lord's coming with patience like that of a farmer. However much we may want the bounty that the earth yields to us, we cannot hasten the cycles of nature. We have no choice but to watch as the soil receives the waters of winter and spring, while we also look forward to the harvest.

The Lord is at hand. Some people take verses like these apart from their context, to support contempt for the world and belief in an imminent violent destruction. But the rest of James's letter refuses to allow us to read these verses so narrowly. It commits us to action for justice *in our world*. We must exercise our patience in the manner of the ancient prophets, doing our best to build justice.

## Gospel: Matthew 11:2–11

*Go...and report...what you hear and see: the blind recover their sight, cripples walk, lepers are cured....*

Skipping over the initial stages of Jesus' ministry, the lectionary directs our attention to Matthew's description of John the Baptizer. From prison, John sends a message to Jesus: "Are you the one who is to come, or should we look for another?" Jesus' answer is indirect: "The blind see, cripples walk, lepers are cured, the deaf hear, the dead are raised to life, and the poor hear the good news. Blest is the one who finds no stumbling-block (offense) in me." This latter statement, which seems to echo the beatitudes, can be viewed as a summary of Jesus' understanding of himself. He is the one who confers citizenship in the reign of God. But he does this always in service of the humblest and most disadvantaged persons. His accomplishments fulfill what prophets, including Isaiah, have foretold.

After dispatching John's messengers, Jesus talks to the crowd about John. The Baptizer is the messenger who has been expected since the time of the prophet Malachi (3:1). But to identify the messenger is also to complete Jesus' identification of himself. In answer to John's question, and to ours: Yes, Jesus is the one who is to come.

## Questions for Reflection

• What evidence in our world tells you that Jesus has been "the one who is to come"? What evidence might persuade you that Jesus has not been the one to come? How is it possible for you to have faith, among all sorts of conflicting evidence?

•What does the question of John the Baptizer contribute to our story of Jesus? What would we miss if this episode were not included? Why do we give the Baptizer more attention at this time of year than at any other time?

•Jesus describes John as prophet, messenger, precursor, and the greatest man born of woman in history, yet also inferior to the least born into God's kingdom. How might Jesus describe you? What might Jesus say publicly about your faith and your zeal for the gospel?

# FOURTH SUNDAY OF ADVENT

## God with us

*[December 24, 1995; December 20, 1998; December 23, 2001]*

### First Reading: Isaiah 7:10–14

*The virgin shall be with child, and bear a son, and shall name him Immanuel.*
The corrupt king Ahaz has been told to look for a sign concerning the
fate of his little kingdom of Judah, and at first he refuses. Speaking
through Isaiah, God has expressed impatience with the king's hypocrisy. The sign is offered: A virgin shall be with child, shall bear a
son, and shall name him Immanuel. Many sources in the Hebrew
Scriptures suggest that Isaiah refers to Ahaz's son Hezekiah, in whom
great hopes are invested.

The subsequent history of the nation of Judah suggests that, however great or virtuous he may have been, Hezekiah could not fulfill
the hopes placed in him. His political alliances and intrigues would, in
Isaiah's analysis, frustrate his otherwise noble reform and sap the
strength of the nation.

Our knowledge of history that could not have been known by the
characters in this text still does not exhaust the power of Isaiah's
imagery. Until the origins of Christianity, many Jews built upon these
verses their hope for a divinely inspired leader who would usher in a
new world. Christians have understood this text to describe the circumstances surrounding the birth of Jesus. Even today we call him
Immanuel, "God with us."

### Responsorial Psalm: Psalm 24:1–2, 3–4, 5–6

### Second Reading: Romans 1:1–7

*Grace and peace from God our Father and Lord Jesus Christ.*
At the beginning of his letter to the fledgling Christian community at
Rome, Paul introduces his purpose in terms of his essential convictions: An apostle is first of all a servant of Christ Jesus. The apostle is
someone set apart to proclaim the gospel. The gospel was promised
long ago by the prophets. The gospel concerns God's Son, a descendant of David. Jesus was made God's Son in power, according to
the spirit of holiness, by his resurrection from the dead.

---

14

In this and in other letters, Paul has refined and clarified these themes. His essential convictions have become ours, for, more than anyone else, Paul is the architect of the Christian faith as we know it. His work has provided a foundation for the gospel accounts of Matthew, Mark, and Luke, all written later in the first century.

This greeting concludes with the apostle's wish for grace and peace upon the church. It is nothing less than Jesus' own gift of peace (John 20:19). As we wait for the Lord, maybe we should examine carefully the ways in which we greet one another.

### Gospel: Matthew 1:18–24

*This is how the birth of Jesus came about.*

There is probably no more famous story in all of world literature. Mary was engaged to Joseph, but the two had not yet lived together. Joseph learned that Mary was pregnant, and, being a decent fellow, he resolved to divorce her quietly, without exposing her to the cruelties of the law. In a dream, Joseph saw an angel who assured him that the child was a gift of the Holy Spirit, a gift who would save people from their sins.

Matthew tells us that these events took place to fulfill the prophecy described in today's first reading. In doing so, he invites us to compare the circumstances into which Hezekiah and Jesus were born. The first is the son of a political ruler, conceived legitimately according to the customs of the time. The second is the son of commoners, conceived in circumstances that could be considered scandalous. Yet history barely remembers Hezekiah, while, for much of humanity, Jesus is the focal point of all history. This is just the first of many ironies embedded in the gospel.

## Questions for Reflection

• How are you called to proclaim the gospel? How do you proclaim the gospel? How can you improve your efforts?

• How do you ordinarily greet people? Do you offer grace and peace, as Paul has done, or do you act in some other way?

• Imagine yourself in Mary's shoes, or in Joseph's. What could assure you that the Holy Spirit was at work in this difficult situation? How do you find the Spirit at work in your various life situations?

# DECEMBER 25, CHRISTMAS, MASS AT MIDNIGHT

*The savior is born*

### First Reading: Isaiah 9:1–6

*For a child is born to us....*

Isaiah heralds the delivery of his people from the grip of Assyria, in terms that contrast utterly with that cruel empire's rule. A great light guides and shines upon the people who have walked in the dark. God has brought them great rejoicing, like that which accompanies the harvest. God has smashed the yoke, the pole, and the rod that have subjugated them. Now the clothes of battle may be burned as fuel.

What is the occasion of all these wonderful and long-awaited things? A child is born to us—a royal child, whose name is Wonderful Counselor, Almighty God, the Everlasting Father, the Prince of Peace. From David's throne he will govern a huge and peaceful kingdom through judgment and justice forever. Our God will do this!

History tells us that, in any literal sense, Isaiah's high hopes were frustrated quickly by continued royal habits of pettiness and short-sightedness. Judah never did find relief from external threat. When at last Assyria was overthrown, Judah was taken into exile by the new power, the Babylonian empire. Any promise of eternal peace and justice might have seemed remote, even a cruel hoax.

But God's promises do not go unfulfilled. The Jews have preserved Isaiah's words not only for their poetic beauty, but because they tell a deep truth. A child will be born to us who will illuminate the darkness that surrounds us. He will rule the world in peace and justice, forever. Christians use these words to announce the birth of Jesus. In many different guises Assyria still threatens us, and peace and justice remain hard to find. Even so, we insist that God has fulfilled the promise spoken by Isaiah. A child is born, and we rejoice.

### Responsorial Psalm: Psalm 96:1–2, 2–3, 11–12, 13

### Second Reading: Titus 2:11–14

*It was he who sacrificed himself for us....*

This text reflects the "already...but not yet" character of our faith. The author summarizes the benefits of God's grace, which offers salvation to all, and which trains us to live in preparation for the glory of God and our Savior Jesus Christ. Jesus has sacrificed himself for us, to save us and to cleanse us for himself. We proclaim a promise kept and, at the same time, a promise yet to be fulfilled. Our savior has come. Yet, with our Jewish cousins, we continue to wait for glory to come.

## Gospel: Luke 2:1–14

*...I come to proclaim good news to you....*

With customary attention to historical detail, Luke describes Joseph arriving in Bethlehem to register himself and Mary in the imperial census. While they remain in Joseph's ancestral home, Mary gives birth to her first-born. She wraps him in swaddling clothes and lays him in a manger. Thus Caesar's and God's purposes collide in an insignificant town in one of the empire's outlying provinces.

Today we are surrounded by the purposes of empire, either Caesar's or Assyria's, or someone else's. But the gospel announces God's purposes, which differ greatly from the purposes of empire. To ensure that we do not overlook the significance of this birth, Luke tells us about shepherds watching their flock nearby in the night. God's angel appears to them as the glory of God bathes them in light, assuring them that they have nothing to fear. The good news is this, says the angel: "A savior has been born to you, the Messiah and Lord. You will find an infant in a manger wrapped in swaddling clothes." Then a "multitude of the heavenly host" appears, shouting "Glory to God. Peace on earth to those whom God favors." A child is born to us, and we rejoice.

## Questions for Reflection

•What empires impose their yokes upon us today? What are some social factors, political realities, and personal habits that cause suffering?

•While empires continue to fight over turf and our allegiances, what sense can it make for us to rejoice?

•What difference does God's grace really make in the world? If we continue to wait for the final glory, what difference does grace make? How?

•What are God's purposes? How do they differ from Caesar's, from Assyria's, from your own habits and expectations?

•The savior is born. How will you rejoice?

# DECEMBER 25, CHRISTMAS, MASS DURING THE DAY

### *The word became flesh*

These readings invite us to reflect on the event described in the midnight Mass gospel. They play a "mystagogical" role, teaching us the significance of mysteries we already know by name and experience.

### First Reading: Isaiah 52:7–10

*All the ends of the earth will behold the salvation of our God.*

The book often called "second Isaiah" comprises chapters 40–55 in our book of Isaiah. It begins with a message of consolation and proceeds to describe and interpret the sufferings of the Lord's servant. It concludes with a portrayal of the Lord's banquet, at which all will fill themselves without cost, and with the promise that God's word will be fulfilled in the chosen people.

These verses describe the work of the servant, the one who brings glad tidings. His feet are beautiful upon the mountains. He announces peace, good news, salvation. He says to Jerusalem, "Your God is King! Pay attention! The watchmen shout for joy, because they can see God restoring Jerusalem. Sing, you who have been ruined, for God comforts and redeems the people. And all the world will know the salvation God has brought."

For Christians, Jesus is the servant, the one whose feet are beautiful on the mountains. He announces peace, good news, salvation, God's kingship, Jerusalem restored.

### Responsorial Psalm: 98:1, 2–3, 3–4, 5–6

### Second Reading: Hebrews 1:1–6

*God...has spoken to us through his Son....*

The author insists that the new revelation is superior in every way to what has gone before. The opening verses teach that, until speaking through the Son, God had spoken in fragmentary and varied fashion. The Son is the agent through whom God has created all things, and the one whose word sustains all created things. Having cleansed us of our sins, the Son has been seated at the Father's right hand. He is superior to the angels.

## Gospel: John 1:1–18
*...enduring love came through Jesus Christ.*

The prologue to John's gospel reminds some observers of the chorus in a Greek drama. Before the drama begins, the chorus provides a context for, and a summary and interpretation of, what is to be presented. It is also intended to invite us into the drama.

To appreciate the power of John's prologue we might envision it setting the stage for the liturgical drama that occurs throughout the seasons of the year. We embark on this familiar journey anew, in order to enter more deeply into the mystery that is the Word among us.

"In the beginning..." chants the chorus, echoing the Bible's very first words. The Word was before all things, and all things came into being through him. The Word was with God and the Word was God. The Word brought light to a darkened and despairing world, and the darkness has never put it out. We should note here that neither has the light (which is the Word) overcome the darkness. We live in between times. The savior has already come, but the final glory awaits.

Perhaps in response to first-century controversies, the prologue insists that John was not the light, but its witness. The light came into the world, and the world did not recognize him. Whoever did accept him has become a child of God. The Word became flesh and pitched his tent among us. We have seen his glory, the glory of a Son filled with enduring love. While the law was a gift through Moses, enduring love came through Jesus Christ. Jesus the Son has revealed God to us.

## Questions for Reflection
• How has Jesus filled the role of God's servant? In what specific ways do you think you have seen Jesus serving God?

• More than a servant, Jesus has also played a vital role in the creation and continued sustenance of the world. Why do the epistle and gospel texts both make this point?

• In what specific ways does the chorus-prelude of John's gospel invite you this year? How have you responded to the drama of the gospel in the past? How will you respond this time around?

• We are bathed in light, surrounded by a dark world. In what ways are we responsible to the world?

• Why does the evangelist insist that no one has ever seen God, right after talking about Moses and the gift of the law? What does this suggest about the relationship between John's community and the Jews of their day? How do you think we should respond to this relationship?

# HOLY FAMILY, SUNDAY IN THE OCTAVE OF CHRISTMAS

## Family harmony

[December 31, 1995; December 27, 1998; December 30, 2001]

### First Reading: Sirach 3:2–6, 12–14

*...kindness to a parent will not be forgotten,...it will take lasting root.*

These verses list the benefits of harmonious family relationships. In particular they praise obedience, expounding on the fourth of the ten commandments. God has set father and mother in positions of honor and authority over their children. To honor one's parents is to be blessed with children, to pray effectively, to live a long life, to obey the Lord. The one who lives by the fourth commandment will reap all manner of blessings as a reward for his or her obedience.

These words typify the work of the author, the Egyptian teacher Yeshua ben Sira, or Sirach. Master of an academy for young Jewish men during the third century before Christ, Sirach was well-traveled and well-educated. Through his lengthy collections of observations on the ways of the world, he sought to demonstrate the superior wisdom of the Jewish way of life: We act wisely when we maintain and revere good relationships with our parents.

### Responsorial Psalm: Psalm 128:1–2, 3, 4–5

### Second Reading: Colossians 3:12–21

*Christ's peace must reign in your hearts.*

What are the habits by which Christians distinguish themselves? This reading lists the major ones. It describes the motives of persons who live in Christian communities, especially in Christian families. The author tells the Colossians that because they are God's chosen ones, they face special obligations. They must bear with one another and forgive one another as God has forgiven them.

The last paragraph of this text sounds a note so jarring that it can ruin the entire passage for many people today. For others, the language poses no problem at all. Wives are told to be submissive to their husbands. Some people find this language offensive and antiquated. Others find it a precise description of a divinely-ordained way of organizing human affairs. This latter position assumes naively that an imperative given to one culture should be imposed upon another, with no attention to nuance or cultural differences.

The virtues and motives listed earlier suggest a clue by which we might understand this paragraph. If we enact the habits that build Christian community, "submission" assumes a secondary importance. More important are mercy, kindness, humility, meekness, patience, forbearance, forgiveness, and most of all, love. Each of us must be submissive to the greater goods of community and mutual love.

### Gospel: Matthew 2, 13–15, 19–23

*...take the child and his mother, and flee to Egypt....*

In a dream, Joseph is told to flee to Egypt to escape the jealous rage of Herod. After Herod's insane crime has been committed, Joseph learns through another dream that it is safe to return to the land of Israel. Fearing Herod's successor, with good reason, Joseph settles the family in Nazareth, in the district of Galilee.

The flight into Egypt reminds us of formative events in Hebrew history. Abram sojourned there (Genesis 12:10–20), and the Hebrew nation was born in its flight from Egypt. Herod's massacre of Israel's first-born, the pivotal event for this text, echoes the tenth plague, but also reverses the miracle of the Passover (Exodus 11:1–12:36). Now, guided almost blindly into actions resembling ancient events, Jesus' family has saved his life. He will live to die in another horrible way, but on behalf of all.

### Questions for Reflection

•How good is your relationship with your parents? What about your relationship with your children? What improvements can you make? How will you make these improvements?

•How do your motives and habits compare to the second reading's list of virtues: mercy, kindness, humility, meekness, patience, forbearance, forgiveness, and love?

•How do you react to the verses about submissiveness? How can we hear them in a manner that builds community, without creating divisions along generational, socio-economic, cultural, or political lines?

• God spoke to Joseph in dreams. How does God seem to speak to you? How can you know what God speaks? How do you respond?

# MARY, MOTHER OF GOD
## JANUARY 1
### *Treasuring*

**First Reading: Numbers 6:22–27**
*The Lord bless you and keep you!*

This text describes a blessing that has become very familiar through its use at Sunday Mass. According to Hebrew tradition, it is a most ancient and solemn blessing, grounded in the unimpeachable authority of Moses. The Lord has told Moses to teach the priests of Israel, Aaron and his descendants, that they must bless Israel in this manner:

May the Lord bless you and keep you!

May the Lord shine the divine face upon you and be gracious to you!

May the Lord look upon you kindly and give you peace!

In each line, a second statement defines and clarifies the first. To wish for God's blessing is also to desire God's protection. God's shining face upon us is related to graciousness, probably best understood as hospitality. And God's kind look upon us is virtually the same thing as the gift of peace.

As we read this text at the beginning of the calendar year, we invite God's protection, graciousness, and peace in all our endeavors.

**Responsorial Psalm: Psalm 67:2–3, 5, 6, 8**

**Second Reading: Galatians 4:4–7**
*You are no longer a slave....*

Paul describes and interprets the birth of God's Son. The verses immediately preceding these assure the audience that they are heirs to the promise given to Abraham long ago, and that common ways of drawing distinctions among people are no longer valid (3:28). Even so, heirs who are under age are not really treated as heirs. They must be supervised. But now God's promise has been kept, in the person of God's Son born of woman. The Son has been born under the law, in order to free the law's subjects. At the appropriate time, the Son has made it possible for all to be God's adopted children. The proof is observable: People who were once as slaves can now cry out *Abba* ("Daddy!"), prompted by the Spirit.

This apparent tautology could lead us into trouble if it were Paul's major point. After all, anyone saying the right words could claim divine justification. In fact, some people did and do act this way. But throughout this letter Paul also challenges the audience to live transformed lives worthy of God's faith in us. Today these verses draw our attention to Mary and invite us to follow her example.

## Gospel: Luke 2:16–21
*Mary treasured all these things and reflected on them in her heart.*
Like all the gospel texts of the season, this one describes a facet of Jesus' infancy. The arrival, departure, and return of shepherds frames and enlarges a tiny scene. Having seen an angel (2:9–13), shepherds rush to Bethlehem, where they find Mary and Joseph, and the baby lying in the manger. They understand what was told to them, and they depart to announce what they have seen and heard. Their activity is a simple and incomplete form of evangelization. It is incomplete because they cannot yet know anything about Christ's passion and resurrection. They have not yet witnessed the gospel. They can tell what they do know, which is that a messenger (angel) has taught them that this child is the long-awaited Messiah, the one who will deliver Israel from bondage. And they can return to the manger, to describe the astonishment that has greeted their news. But they cannot really understand.

We should contrast their actions with those of the child's mother. Mary knows no more about the trajectory of Jesus' life than the shepherds, but she has been privileged with a deeper knowledge. The child is God's son. She treasures this secret and all these other things, and reflects upon them in her heart.

Like the shepherds, we must respond to the great gift of Christmas. Like Mary, we must also treasure all that has been revealed to us. Lacking this deeper awareness, our words and actions might astonish, but they could not announce the gospel.

## Questions for Reflection
•How does God bless you? How does God shine the divine face on you? In what kind ways does God look upon you?

•How do you address God? How often do you use a comfortable, familiar term like "Daddy"? What is keeping you from speaking to God in this way more often?

•What do you treasure and reflect upon in your heart?

•How do you announce the good news? How do people respond to you?

•How will you celebrate Christmas in contemplation and action?

# EPIPHANY

## Your light has come

[January 7, 1996; January 3, 1999; January 6, 2002]

### First Reading: Isaiah 60:1–6

*...upon you the Lord shines....*

In pitch darkness, even the merest pinpoint of light offers comfort and the promise of safety. Amid the darkness that covers the earth, Jerusalem is illuminated in the glory of the Lord. The divine light shall guide nations and their kings, and indeed all the peoples of the earth. From the ends of the earth people will come bearing gifts, guided by the light that is the Lord's glory.

An anonymous poet whose work is included in our book of Isaiah speaks to a generation returned from exile. This text invites us to stand beside the chosen people, newly restored to their homeland, to look into the darkness from a brilliantly lit place. See, says the prophet, all the nations of the earth walk by your light, and they come to you.

For us, the most interesting gifts are named in the final verse: Travelers from Sheba shall bear gold and frankincense. Today's gospel adds to these myrrh, a burial spice. Christians insist that Jesus has taken on the blessings and the responsibilities of the chosen people. He has done this by dying and rising. He has endowed his followers with his own glory, and with his own responsibilities.

### Responsorial Psalm: Psalm 72:1–2, 7–8, 10–11, 12–13

### Second Reading: Ephesians 3:2–3, 5–6

*...the Gentiles are now co-heirs....*

The author insists that in Christ Jesus the Gentiles are now co-heirs with the Jews, members of the same body and sharers of the same promise given to Abraham and his descendants. We must not overlook the double irony. First, the Christian claim to Israel's promise is, from a Jewish perspective, brusque, undiplomatic, outrageous. How would you like it if a stranger tried to claim your identity? How would you feel if you caught someone else wearing your clothes, mimicking your speech, affecting your mannerisms, claiming even your family?

Second, the author of this letter, who is not Paul, nonetheless writes in Paul's name. Pseudonymous writing was common in ancient literature, as today's first reading also illustrates. This author probably never had a second thought about writing under Paul's identity, nor about Christians claiming the inheritance of the Jews. But on this festival of light piercing the darkness we must think twice. If we are to be co-heirs, let us not forget the illuminated audience of the first reading, who were heirs to God's promises before we were.

### Gospel: Matthew 2:1–12
*They prostrated themselves and did him homage.*

An epiphany is a revelation of the divine. Since early Christian centuries, Matthew's tale of visitors from the east has focused our celebration of God's self-disclosure before all the world. In the first reading, God is revealed in the people of Israel. Here, pagan wise men, who represent all the nations of the world, see God in the face of the infant under the light of a star.

The story is familiar throughout the world. Mysterious visitors from the orient follow a star to the stable that is the first home of the "new-born king of Israel." First dropping in on Herod, eventually they find their way to Bethlehem where they present to the infant Jesus gifts of gold, frankincense, and myrrh.

Epiphany, the culmination of Christmas, illustrates perfectly the revolutionary nature of our faith. With the rest of the world, we long for images of royalty and the trappings of privilege. Here, these images stood on their heads. Visitors bearing fabulous wealth brave untold miles and a jealous king to gaze into the face of a baby. This baby is the light who guides our world through the dark. He bathes us in the brilliant light that is God's glory, while also placing upon us serious ethical and social responsibilities. Like our cousins the Jews, we are examples for the rest of the world. Our king is born, and our star is rising. Let us live up to our calling.

### Questions for Reflection

•In what ways has God fulfilled promises made to you? In turn, what are some of your responsibilities?

•What is your attitude toward people of other faiths in general, and toward the Jewish people in particular? How do these readings challenge your attitudes? How do they affirm them?

•What do you do to reveal God's glory to others? How might you begin to do this, if you do not already do so?

# BAPTISM OF THE LORD

## Fulfilling what God requires

[January 8 (Monday) 1996 ; January 10, 1999; January 13, 2002]

### First Reading: Isaiah 42:1–4, 6–7

*Here is my servant, whom I uphold....*

This is the first of the four "servant songs," which are the work of the mysterious prophet known as "second Isaiah." Presenting the servant, the Lord's voice insists that justice is the core of the servant's mission. The servant will open the eyes of the blind, bring out prisoners from confinement, and lead into light those who live in darkness. The servant is the one upon whom God has placed the divine spirit, the one who will bring justice to the nations. The servant shall not cry out in the street, nor break a bruised reed nor quench a smoldering wick, until justice is established throughout the earth. God has called the servant for the victory of justice, taken the servant by the hand, and formed the servant as a covenant, a light for all peoples.

From the beginning the identity of the servant has been ambiguous. Was the servant a contemporary of the Jews returned from captivity? Was the servant a "messiah" (anointed one) yet to come? Was the servant the Jewish people themselves? All these answers are possible. But one thing remains clear: The servant brings justice to the earth. We recognize the servant through his or her establishment of justice, in the blind receiving sight, in the release of captives, and in light given to those in the dark.

### Responsorial Psalm: Psalm 29:1–2, 3–4, 3, 9–10

### Second Reading: Acts of the Apostles 10:34–38

*...God anointed him with the Holy Spirit and power.*

Peter preached one of the first Christian homilies to a group assembled at the home of a Roman centurion. Cornelius has just seen a vision of a man in dazzling robes, which reminds us of what the women witnessed at Jesus' empty tomb (Luke 24:4; Acts 10:30ff). The vision has told Cornelius to cross all cultural boundaries and to invite Simon Peter to his house. For his part, Peter has also had a vision (10:9–16), which insists that God alone decides what or who is clean.

In this extraordinary encounter, Peter preaches and the whole household is baptized. Peter explains this action to his astonished companions by insisting that the Holy Spirit has descended upon these Gentiles, as the Spirit had filled the Twelve on Pentecost day.

These verses give us the first half of Peter's homily. He has discovered that God shows no partiality. Anyone who fears God and acts uprightly is acceptable to God. Speaking to his audience as foreigners, Peter knows that they have heard about Jesus of Nazareth, but still he begins a summary of the gospel. Intentionally incomplete, this reading reminds us of the drama, risks, and demands of Christian baptism.

## Gospel: Matthew 3:13–17
*This is my beloved Son. My favor rests on him.*

The Christmas season concludes today. The fact of Jesus' baptism is likely to have been an embarrassment to the first-century church. After all, why would the one who is without sin undergo a purifying bath that washes sin away?

Matthew's narrative provides an explanation that contributes to his larger theological perspective. Here, John the Baptizer at first tries to refuse Jesus with the words "I should be baptized by you." Yet the baptism must be done, to *fulfill* God's demands. With this encounter Matthew sets a pattern. Throughout this gospel account Jesus fulfills the law, tradition, and God's expectations. He has remade baptism in terms of his death and resurrection. Today, the church intends that we also recognize Jesus fulfilling the ancient "servant's" mission of justice.

In a description common to Matthew, Mark, and Luke, Jesus emerges from the water and the sky opens. The Spirit of God descends like a dove over Jesus, and a heavenly voice says, "This is my beloved Son. My favor rests on him."

## Questions for Reflection

•How might we recognize the servant's activity in the world? What has the servant already accomplished? What work remains undone?

•Under what conditions were you baptized? How does the drama of Cornelius's baptism compare or contrast with yours? What are your baptismal responsibilities? How are they like those of the first Christians?

•Upon whom does God's favor rest? When was the last time you felt God's favor upon you? How often do you feel this way? What does God require of you?

# ASH WEDNESDAY

*Return*

*[February 21, 1996; February 17, 1999; February 20, 2002]*

### First Reading: Joel 2:12–18

*Rend your hearts, not your garments....*

At the most elemental level, Lent is our annual invitation to return to the Lord. This text frames the invitation in explicit and dramatic terms. With it we describe the shape of our entire lenten journey.

"Return to me with your whole heart," says the Lord, "in fasting, weeping, and mourning. Rend your hearts, not your garments. Return to our God, who is merciful and gracious. Blow the trumpet, proclaim a fast, assemble all the people, including officials and infants and every-one in between. Even the bride and groom must quit their chamber to join all the people. On our behalf the priests will pray, 'Spare us, Lord.'"

We might not feel the peril implied in these words. Our lives might be so filled with material comforts and success that we rarely think about loss or deprivation. By contrast, Joel's audience had endured a devastating plague of locusts that compelled them to look inward and to seek God's forgiveness. Today's text concludes the prophet's graphic descriptions of Israel's suffering. It also inaugurates the more hopeful second half of this short book with the final verse: "The Lord was moved to care for the land and took pity on the people."

Our lives are surely more fragile than we imagine. Our only real security rests in God, and yet we too easily place our hopes in other things. In fact, if not in name, we drift away from God, taking our hopes to the altars of lesser, inadequate gods. Return to the Lord who is gracious and merciful, who is kind and who forgives. Return.

### Responsorial Psalm: Psalm 51:3–4, 5–6, 12–13, 14, 17

### Second Reading: 2 Corinthians 5:20–6:2

*Now is the day of salvation!*

Paul reminds us of our responsibilities to one another and to the world. We are ambassadors for Christ. In a sense, what we do reflects upon God. Because the stakes are so high, Paul speaks passionately: "I beg you, in Christ's name, be reconciled to God!"

Because of Christ, we can become holy. Let us not receive this enormous grace in vain. Paul reminds us of the prophecy: "In an acceptable time I hear you; On a day of salvation I hear you" (Isaiah 49:8). He also makes a stronger point: Now is the acceptable time! Now is the day of salvation!

## Matthew 6:1–6, 16–18

*...your Father who sees in secret will repay you.*

The sermon on the mount occupies chapters 5 through 7 in Matthew's account of the gospel. The first half of chapter 6 summarizes Jesus' teaching about prayer and other specifically "religious" disciplines. Here we have most of that material, excluding the Lord's prayer.

As in the rest of the sermon, Jesus desires good motives even as he expresses disdain for appearances. He seems to dismiss as hypocrisy any good act that draws attention. Do not let others see your religious acts, he says. Assist the poor quietly and without fanfare. Keep secret the merciful actions you perform. Do not pray like hypocrites, in public. Instead, go to your room and pray in private. Neither should you fast as hypocrites do. Instead, groom your hair and wash your face, so that only your Father can see.

This text accompanies the distribution of ashes, through which we mark ourselves as Christians embarking upon Lent. Together, these three readings put each one of us on the spot. We are invited to return. We are challenged to live up to the grace that has been given to us. And we are told to avoid the appearance of hypocrisy, even as we mark ourselves. We must rend our hearts, not our garments.

## Questions for Reflection

•What dangers do you fear? Where do you turn for security? Where can you find real hope? What must you do to return to God?

•In what ways are you responsible to others? How are you and your fellow Christians responsible to the world? What will you do to accept and enact a deepened sense of responsibility during this season?

•Why do we mark ourselves with ashes right after reading Jesus' cautionary teaching about appearances? How can we justify this practice?

•How do you pray? What do you hope to accomplish when you fast, assist the poor, and give mercy? Why do you do these things? Who can see you doing them?

•What changes must you make to return to the Lord?

# FIRST SUNDAY OF LENT

## The tempter

[February 25, 1996; February 21, 1999; February 24, 2002]

Lent originated early in the history of the church as a final preparation for the baptism of new Christians. Essentially a long retreat, Lent brought to a focused conclusion the lengthy period of preparation known as the *catechumenate*. During Lent catechumens were required to pray, fast, and assist the poor, in the midst of and supported by the Christian community. Their journeys climaxed at Easter when, after vigiling through the night, the new Christians were baptized and anointed at the break of dawn. Then, for the first time, they joined the community at the Lord's table.

The catechumenate was restored by Vatican Council II. On the first Sunday of Lent parishes celebrate the first of several communal rites leading toward Easter baptisms. This is the Rite of Election, or the Rite of Enrollment of Names. Often in the presence of the bishop, the community recognizes, examines, and prays over the catechumens, now called "elect," immediately following the liturgy of the word. The elect are living, breathing reminders that God invites us all to return.

### First Reading: Genesis 2:7–9; 3:1–7

*...so man became a living being.*

To say that Lent is our annual invitation to return to God is to acknowledge that we have turned away. God has made all people essentially good, but sometimes we fail to do what is good and right. During Lent we must recognize that we are tempted, and that sometimes we give in to temptation.

One character seems to dominate all three of these readings. Known variously as serpent, tempter, and Satan, he represents the human capacity to sin. His presence in the early chapters of Genesis illustrates the sophisticated manner in which the ancient Hebrews confronted the problem of evil. This problem remains with us today. Like our ancestors, we must wrestle daily with the fact that we can and do introduce evil into a good world made by a good God.

This reading allows us to glimpse two different facets of the second story of creation, which follows the first creation story in Genesis. God has formed the human person as the crowning achievement in all creation. When we sin, however, we isolate ourselves from God, from others, and from creation. We make excuses and alibis, and we try to remake ourselves in the images of other, lesser gods.

### Responsorial Psalm: Psalm 51:3–4, 5–6, 12–13, 14, 17

### Second Reading: Romans 5:12–19
*...through one man's obedience all shall become just.*
Paul presents the core of Christian theology. In a tightly-reasoned passage, he contrasts the offense of Adam with Christ's redemptive death and resurrection. If sin has entered the world through the disobedience of one man, Christ's obedient acceptance of the cross has canceled any claim that sin might try to impose on us.

### Gospel: Matthew 4:1–11
*...God alone shall you adore.*
Three temptations beset the freshly baptized Jesus in the desert. The first reminds him of his hunger, and therefore of all his appetites and desires. It tells him to take care of himself, thereby proving that he is the Son of God. The second swings wildly in the opposite direction, daring him to throw himself off the temple parapet, and to test God's protection. The third is the most dangerous, because all the kingdoms of the world should, it would seem, belong to someone who is the Son of God.

Jesus resists and cites a verse from the Scriptures each time he fends off the tempter. His response to the third temptation is decisive, as he reverses the theological crisis portrayed in today's first reading. Citing Deuteronomy 6:13, Jesus stands in the desert, empty. He has abandoned his hungers and his dreams, and now he clings to the hope that a God who is bigger than any human imagining will make everything right. This is the obedience of which Paul has spoken, a trust in the fundamental goodness of God, the human person, and creation. It is also the model for what we must do during Lent, and always.

### Questions for Reflection
•How often do you savor your essential goodness? What obstacles sometimes make this difficult for you?

•What are your biggest temptations?

•How will you enter the desert during Lent? How will you deal with your temptations? What discipline will you follow? To whom will you turn for help?

# SECOND SUNDAY OF LENT

## Holiness

*[March 3, 1996; February 28, 1999; March 3, 2002]*

### First Reading: Genesis 12:1–4

*...I will bless you.*

In the reckoning of most scholars, the call of Abram is the first historical event narrated in the Bible. By virtue of resemblances to, and contrasts with, ancient Mesopotamian and Palestinian tales, the stories in the first eleven chapters of Genesis present Israel's distinctive spin on the creation of the world, the origins of humanity, and pre-historical events remembered dimly by all ancient cultures, especially the great flood.

Beginning with chapter 12 we are immersed in a long narrative that tells of initial and continuing encounters between Abram and God. Today's story opens in Mesopotamia, modern Iraq, when Abram hears the voice of a God unlike any other. This God tells him to leave his family and the civilization he has known all his life and to settle in "a land that I will show you." Abram obeys the voice of this previously unknown God, and leaves his native land.

### Responsorial Psalm: Psalm 33:4–5, 18–19, 20, 22

### Second Reading: 2 Timothy 1:8–10

*He has robbed death of its power....*

According to the author of this letter, probably not Paul, all Christians have been called to a holy life. We have not merited our call. God's grace and blessing are offered in Christ Jesus, who has robbed death of its power and illuminated life with the gospel.

### Gospel: Matthew 17:1–9

*Get up! Do not be afraid.*

There are two points in Matthew's account of the gospel at which a voice from the heavens identifies Jesus as "my beloved son, on whom my favor rests." The first is at Jesus' baptism (3:17), and the second is at the transfiguration, described in this text. At a third and related

32

point, the voices of Roman observers identify Jesus as the Son of God, when he dies on the cross (27:54). For Matthew, these three points belong together. The baptism and crucifixion are distinct facets in Christ's single act of salvation, while the transfiguration is a foretaste of Christ's resurrection. It completes and interprets the other two points.

Matthew describes the transfiguration like this: Jesus takes Peter, James, and John high up on a mountain, apart from the others. His face becomes as dazzling as the sun, his clothes like light. Moses and Elijah, the other great mountaintop prophets, appear, and they converse with Jesus. Peter responds to these extraordinary things with the suggestion that he build three booths, as if for the Jewish feast of Tabernacles (Succoth), one each for Jesus, Moses, and Elijah. But before he can finish speaking a bright cloud overshadows all, and a voice from the cloud says, "This is my beloved Son. Listen to him." The disciples fall to the ground in fear, but Jesus urges them to get up and not be afraid. Looking around, the disciples see only Jesus, who touches them and commands them not to tell anyone of this vision until the Son of Man has risen from the dead.

Like other messengers who guide frail human beings through the terrifying spectacles that sometimes mark divine appearances, Jesus tells the disciples that they must not fear. But unlike any other messenger, Jesus is himself the center of the spectacle. He is God's Son, in all ways like God.

We must not allow the spectacle to overshadow a more subtle and very important point. In its way, each of these readings calls us to holiness. The epistle does so in a simple and straightforward way, while the first reading narrates the very beginning of human holiness. The gospel reminds us that we must not fear God, who is both one of us and a mysterious, dazzling Other. To return to God is to become holy.

## Questions for Reflection

•How has God called you? What has God called upon you to do? How have you responded?

•What is holiness? What does Abram's story suggest concerning holiness? What does the gospel text suggest?

•How do you listen for Jesus' voice?

•What do you fear? What does Jesus say to you, concerning each of your fears?

# THIRD SUNDAY OF LENT

## Thirsts

*[March 10, 1996; March 7, 1999; March 10, 2002]*

The scrutinies are celebrated on the third, fourth, and fifth Sundays of Lent. These are rites in which the elect (see Rite of Election, first Sunday of Lent) stand before the community, who pray with and for them, in order that any remaining impediments to the gospel may be removed from their lives. In each scrutiny, elect and community together examine their consciences and acknowledge publicly that they have sinned. The scrutinies are not, however, public confession. Nor are they about guilt. Rather, these rites require that Christians and elect scrutinize all of their behavior over against the love of Jesus Christ. They cause us to face some hard questions. The scrutinies are the primary means through which the community directs and supports the elect as they continue their long lenten retreat. They are also a powerful directive and support for the Christian faithful.

The first scrutiny is celebrated on the third Sunday of Lent. Its prayers and symbols embody our radical dependence upon the living water that Jesus offers. It is always to be prefaced by a proclamation of John 4. That is why church law directs that every parish hosting even one elect must proclaim the year A gospel, even in years B and C.

### First Reading: Exodus 17:3–7

*I will be standing there in front of you....*

Long after the excitement of their escape has worn off, the people grumble against Moses. Their thirst drives them to wonder what good their freedom can be, if they are merely going to die in the desert. God instructs Moses to strike a rock with his staff. Water will flow for people to drink. Moses follows the instructions, and the place receives a name commemorating the Israelites' quarreling and testing.

### Responsorial Psalm: Psalm 95:1–2, 6–7, 8–9

### Second Reading: Romans 5:1–2, 5–8

*Christ died for us.*

The significance of the water featured in the other two readings is made explicit in these verses about the abundant, overflowing, life-

34

giving grace that has been poured into our hearts through the Spirit. Christ's death on our behalf is the foundation for our hope, our faith, the grace and love given to us, and the continued sustenance of the Spirit.

## Gospel: John 4:5–42

*...whoever drinks the water I give...will never be thirsty....*

Traveling through Samaria, Jesus arrives one day at noon at the site of Jacob's well. A woman approaches, and Jesus asks her for water. What follows is a dialog in which the woman begins by toying with Jesus. Before long, however, she can see that he knows her better than she knows herself, and she drops all her defenses. She runs off to invite many of her acquaintances to come and hear Jesus for themselves, and she returns with a crowd. Many hear for themselves, and they believe.

The dialog between Jesus and the woman uses the common experience of thirst to represent all the deepest yearnings of the human heart. The woman wants water, so she totes a bucket in the noonday sun. She wants love, so she has married five men and now consorts with a sixth. She wants religious truth, so she debates with Jesus about remembered stories common to Samaritan and Jew. Jesus accompanies her as she expresses her yearnings, and he promises to satisfy each one. He looks into her soul and tells her everything she ever did. She comes to know that he really can give living water.

The ironies in the story strip away all of our pretenses, too. It is the Samaritan, the despised sibling, who believes. As if to sharpen the point, a whole community of Samaritans comes into faith while the privileged disciples miss everything. A response to a simple request for a drink becomes a life-changing act of hospitality. Barriers drawn by gender, social standing, nationality, and religion are stripped away, so that only worship in Spirit and truth remain. With this text we proclaim Jesus standing before us insisting, "Give me a drink."

## Questions for Reflection

•When were you really thirsty? What was it like? What satisfied your thirst?

•When did Jesus most recently ask you for a drink? How did he ask, and through whom? How did you respond?

•How would you relate to someone who knows all of your secrets?

•What is worship in Spirit and truth? In what ways does it differ from your usual ways of praying, of thinking, of behaving?

# FOURTH SUNDAY OF LENT

*Seeing*

*[March 17, 1996; March 14, 1999; March 17, 2002]*

### First Reading: 1 Samuel 16:1b, 6–7, 10–13a

*...the Lord looks into the heart.*

Saul, the first king of Israel, is paranoid and probably insane. He must be replaced, and the Lord has told Samuel to anoint one of the sons of Jesse. To elude Saul's suspicions, Samuel travels under the pretext of performing a sacrifice, taking a heifer to Bethlehem.

Reviewing each of the sons, Samuel guesses incorrectly. At last Jesse summons the youngest, and the Lord tells Samuel that this David will be king. God does not see as we see, because we look at appearances, while God looks into the heart.

### Responsorial Psalm: Psalm 23:1–3, 3–4, 5, 6

### Second Reading: Ephesians 5:8–14

*...now you are light in the Lord.*

The author of this letter (almost certainly not Paul) introduces a simple and powerful image. The Christians at Ephesus once dwelt in darkness, but now they are children of light. Light produces every kind of goodness and justice and truth, while "vain deeds done in darkness" must produce evil, injustice, and falsehood.

The reading concludes with a formula prayer that was probably well-known to the original audience: "Awake, O sleeper, arise from the dead, and Christ will give you light." Most scholars agree that these words were pronounced at many early baptism liturgies.

### Gospel: John 9:1–41

*I am the light of the world.*

Jesus gives sight to a man born blind. This simple and yet astonishing act lies at the core of a drama exploring the struggle between light and darkness, a major theme in John's gospel, and the focus of the second scrutiny. Here Jesus, the light of the world, wins several victories over darkness. First, he accomplishes a healing unparalleled in ancient times. Second, he illustrates the overwhelming power of God's glory, vanquishing sin, which stands no chance. Third, the behavior of authorities shows them to remain, in every way, in the dark.

Encountering a man blind since birth, the disciples ask Jesus a legalistic question. Is he blind because of his sin, or because of a sin of his ancestors (see Exodus 20:5)? Jesus introduces a third possibility, that the man is blind so that God's works might be revealed in him. Then, spitting on the ground, he makes mud, which he rubs on the man's eyes. When the man obeys Jesus' order to wash, he sees.

The man's troubles have just begun. Astonished neighbors demand an explanation. He can only offer a simple description of his experience. The neighbors take him to the authorities who debate the theological significance of the miracle, question the man's parents, and interrogate the man a second time. Placing Jesus on trial by proxy, they demand to hear the man's story again. He states explicitly the drama's central point: "You do not know who Jesus is, but only God can accomplish what he has done." In a final scene, the man sees Jesus for the first time. Professing his belief, he bows in worship.

It is unfortunate that John's gospel casts Jesus' victory over the authorities in anti-Jewish terms. Today we must recognize this bias and correct similar tendencies in ourselves. To perpetuate anti-Jewishness or any other form of racism is to dwell in precisely the darkness that Jesus has cast out.

This story connects light, life, and baptism. To refuse to believe is to remain in darkness, to continue in sin; but to believe is to see. The story also makes a subtle point. To be sure, God's works are revealed when the man washes his eyes in the pool. But they are revealed more clearly as he narrates his experience and grows into a profession of faith.

The second scrutiny invites us to allow Christ's light to illuminate every last nook and cranny in our lives. It celebrates the miracle of light in our lives, and the even greater miracle of the elect professing their faith before the world. It insists that we stop pretending to see when we do not, and to open our eyes.

## Questions for Reflection

•What are your "deeds done in darkness"? What are you called to do about them?

•How and where did your faith begin? How was your faith tested early, and how have you been tested more recently?

•How do you see God working, in the lives of people around you, and in your own life?

# FIFTH SUNDAY OF LENT

*Spirit and life*

[March 24, 1996; March 21, 1999; March 24, 2002]

### First Reading: Ezekiel 37:12–14

*Then you shall know that I am the Lord.*

The visionary prophet Ezekiel is led by the hand of the Lord into a plain filled with bones. Instructed to call out to the bones, he follows instructions and witnesses some of the most astonishing events portrayed anywhere in the world's literature. Bone joins upon bone, sinews upon skeleton, flesh upon sinew, and skin upon flesh. Most important, God commands "spirit" to enter those who have been slain, and Ezekiel beholds an army. These visions are interpreted. The bones are the people of Israel, soon to return from exile. These verses issue God's climactic promise: "I will open your graves and command you to rise from them. I will place my spirit in you and settle you upon your land."

### Responsorial Psalm: Psalm 130:1–2, 3–4, 5–6, 7–8

### Second Reading: Romans 8:8–11

*...the Spirit of God dwells in you.*

Paul distinguishes between "flesh" and "spirit." Anyone "in the flesh" cannot please God. But Paul's audience is "in the spirit." If Christ is in you, the body is dead because of sin.

On first glance, we might think that these verses devalue our human bodies and our interactions with the world around us. But the last verse insists that the one who raised Christ from the dead will bring our mortal bodies to life also, through the Spirit dwelling within us. To be "in the spirit" is to value our bodies, our whole lives, and the whole lives of others.

How can we be in the spirit? The strongest clue is Paul's insistence that the spirit lives because of justice. But justice occurs in earthy, embodied situations: It cannot be abstract. For example, we do justice when we feed the hungry and when we give shelter to the homeless person. We also do justice when we help the hungry and the homeless to provide for themselves. To be in the spirit is to work always for justice, animated by God's own Spirit. It is to keep the promises we made, or which were made on our behalf, or which we will make very soon at Easter, at our baptisms.

## Gospel: John 11:1–45

*I am the resurrection and the life.*

Lazarus has died, and his friend Jesus is led to the burial place. Troubled in spirit and moved by the deepest emotions, Jesus directs the stone to be moved from the tomb. He offers a prayer of thanksgiving (*eucharisto*) to the Father and calls Lazarus out. As the first reading illustrates, only God can do such a thing.

This story climaxes the cycle of stories that accompany the scrutinies. Truths represented metaphorically in the stories of the Samaritan woman and the man born blind are made explicit in this one. Jesus, who gives living water and light, also brings the dead to life. Jesus fills our deepest yearnings and illumines the darkest recesses of our souls. Most important, he brings life to the most hopeless and seemingly irreversible situations.

This is the core of our faith. Doctrines and creeds express realities that transform the lives of those who profess those words. But doctrines and creeds are not themselves these transforming realities. Words alone accomplish little, and too often we only pronounce the words. Sometimes we resist Christ's genuine and constant offer of life. Sometimes we live in the flesh, not in the spirit.

This story also illustrates the role of the community in the faith of the individual person. God alone gives life and faith and satisfies our deepest thirsts. Still, the community must unbind the person who has been set free. In this important respect, the story of Lazarus contrasts with that of the man born blind. In the latter story, the man comes into faith despite being abandoned by neighbors, parents, and authorities. Here we see a community responding properly to Jesus' gift of life, and we are challenged to act in a similar manner.

## Questions for Reflection

•What dead ends do you encounter? What situations do you find most rigid, hopeless, irreversible? How often do you ask God to bring life to these situations?

•In what ways do you sometimes impose limits upon God's work? How does your parish inhibit God's work? How do your neighborhood, your town, your society frustrate God's intentions? What can you do about these limitations? What will you do about them?

•When and how do you give thanks to God?

# PASSION SUNDAY (PALM SUNDAY)

## *The Cross*

*[March 31, 1996; March 28, 1999; March 31, 2002]*

### Procession: Matthew 21:1–11

*Blessed be the one who comes in the name of the Lord!*

We enter the great drama of Christ's passion by reenacting the story of Jesus' entry into Jerusalem. We distribute palms and process. We join our ancestors in shouting, "Hosanna: God save him." Unlike them, however, we cannot remain spectators. This is our drama, the center of our lives. Today we embark again on the journey to the cross.

### First Reading: Isaiah 50:4–7

*The Lord God is my hope.*

The church has always viewed Jesus as the "suffering servant" of Second Isaiah. That book's third servant song sets the tone for today's long gospel proclamation. The servant has used God-given gifts in a faithful manner, teaching, healing, and assisting others. And when asked to suffer, the servant has submitted.

The closing verse offers a hint of the glory of the cross: "The Lord God is my help, therefore I am not disgraced; I have set my face like flint, knowing that I shall not be put to shame."

### Responsorial Psalm: Psalm 22:8–9, 17–18, 19–20, 23–24

### Second Reading: Philippians 2:6–11

*God highly exalted him.*

These verses constitute one of the very first Christian hymns. Probably sung at some early liturgies, the hymn proclaims our most basic beliefs. Christ is God's equal, but he emptied himself, having been born in our likeness. As one of us, he accepted everything that came his way, even death on the cross. And because of this obedient death, God has glorified Jesus and directed all creation to worship him.

We too must empty ourselves, allow ourselves to be humbled, and accept suffering as we serve our God and all of God's creatures.

## Gospel: Matthew 26:14–27:66
*Take this and eat it. This is my body.*

The passion narrative is the core of each account of the gospel. Evidence suggests that the story of Jesus' death was told and retold in a standard form before other traditions about Jesus took shape. This form includes a description of the Last Supper, at which Jesus gives the Eucharist to the church. It also describes the departure of Judas, Jesus' impassioned prayer in the garden, and his arrest there. It portrays his trials before Herod and Pontius Pilate, and his condemnation. It describes his cross-burdened walk to Calvary, his crucifixion among criminals, his death, and his burial. Toward the end of the first century, authors including Mark, Matthew, Luke, and John created accounts of the gospel by weaving various orally transmitted traditions around the central passion story.

Because each author emphasized distinct literary and theological points, we can find differences and even disagreements among the various accounts. Matthew's passion story includes all the material set forth in Mark's earlier version and adds the death of Judas and Jesus' concern for "fulfilling the scriptures" (26:52–54 and 56). It gives Pilate a larger role than do Mark or Luke, and it absolves Pilate for Jesus' condemnation while blaming Jesus' own people (27:24–25). Alone among the passion stories, Matthew's version describes an earthquake and the raisings of dead saints at the moment of Jesus' death.

The differences among the passion stories should not disturb us, because they are not intended to be factual reports, in our modern sense. Matthew's passion tells far more than history. It defines us and our way of life. Today we read the passion as drama to accentuate the truths we celebrate at every Eucharist: We are the ones whom Jesus nourishes, who follow his example, who are called to the cross.

### Questions

•Why is it important that you enter into and participate in the drama of the passion? Why shouldn't you remain a spectator?

•How does your attitude resemble Christ's? How does your attitude differ from Christ's? How must you change? How will you change?

•What role best fits you in the drama that is Christ's passion? Would you be Jesus, or Pilate, or Peter, or Judas, or someone else? Why does this role fit you better than others?

•What cross do you carry? How do you carry it? What help do you enlist? What additional help do you need?

# CHRISM MASS

*[Ordinarily on Holy Thursday, the Chrism Mass is scheduled by the bishop*
*between Passion Sunday and the Mass of the Lord's Supper.*
*Holy Thursday: April 4, 1996; April 1, 1999; April 4, 2002]*

Each year, the priests and people of every diocese gather with their bishops. The priests renew their commitment to ordained ministry and concelebrate the Eucharist, and all witness the consecration of the holy oils. The Chrism Mass is a feast of symbols, and a final preparation for the climactic celebrations of the Easter Triduum.

The symbols embodied at this Mass follow ancient practice. The oil to be used for sacramental anointing is blessed first; the oil of catechumens follows. It is to be used for exorcisms and to strengthen catechumens in public rites as they journey toward Easter. Lastly, the bishop consecrates Chrism. Having mixed balsam or other perfume into the oil, he breathes upon the mixture and recites a prayer evoking the place of oil at crucial points in Hebrew and Christian history. This prayer also reminds us of connections between oil and water. Chrism is to be used to anoint neophytes at their baptisms, and for all other confirmations. It is also used to anoint the hands of priests when they are ordained.

However powerful, these rites are purposely incomplete. They set the stage for our Easter celebration. Because priests are servants, the renewal of their priesthood is fulfilled out among the faithful. Because we are all God's servants, our annual renewal thrusts us out into a world hungry for the gospel.

## First Reading: Isaiah 61:1–3, 6, 8–9
*You yourselves shall be named priests of the Lord.*

These verses from the third, pseudonymously written portion of the book of Isaiah record a speech delivered by the one who has been anointed. The first verse describes the inherent connections between God's spirit and a person, and God's anointing. The anointing has a purpose: "to bring glad tidings … heal … proclaim liberty … and release … announce a year of favor … comfort … give a glorious mantle." The anointed is not identified by the author. He or she may be the entire community of Israel recently returned from exile. We might call the servant an "enabler." Moreover, the whole congregation, modern as well as ancient, hears the divine intent: "You are priests...ministers, exemplars before your children and the nations of the world." We may find in these words a job description for our priests, but also for the whole church.

## Responsorial Psalm: Psalm 89:21–22, 25, 27

## Second Reading: Revelation 1:5–8
*I am the Alpha and the Omega.*

These verses sound more like Paul than the fiery, visionary tone of most of the book. They comprise a portion of the introduction, and, like the first reading, they define the audience as a "priestly people." Here the agent of God's anointing is Jesus Christ, the first-born from the dead and the ruler of all kings. Jesus anoints, especially through his sacrifice. An apocalyptic tone emerges in verse 7, which echoes Daniel 7:13 and Zechariah 12:10: "Look, he is coming among the clouds, and everyone will see him, even those who killed him."

## Gospel: Luke 4,16–21
*The spirit of the Lord is upon me....*

After his baptism and after facing down the devil in a long retreat in the desert, Jesus begins his public life. Here we see him returned to his home synagogue at Nazareth, where his emerging reputation has preceded him (4:14–15). He reads exactly those verses that constitute today's first reading. He begins a sermon that will end with his expulsion from the synagogue (4:28–30) with the matter-of-fact statement, "Today this passage is fulfilled in your presence."

Jesus' example is audacious, even offensive to some. It is exactly this audacity that seals his fate later, when he faces the Sanhedrin in Jerusalem (22:71). The Easter Triduum celebrates Jesus' unwavering faithfulness to the anointed's ancient purpose. His priestly people are called to a similar audacity, invited into the same purpose.

## Questions for Reflection

•To whom do you bear glad tidings? Whom do you heal? On whose behalf do you proclaim liberty?

•How can you improve the way in which you meet these responsibilities? What specific steps will you take right away?

•Reflect upon these readings as a way of renewing your own vocation. How will you prepare to celebrate this renewal through the Easter Triduum? What sort of assistance do you need to accomplish your renewal?

# EASTER TRIDUUM
## HOLY THURSDAY,
## MASS OF THE LORD'S SUPPER

### *Servanthood*

*[April 4, 1996; April 1, 1999; April 4, 2002]*

### First Reading: Exodus 12:1–8, 11–14

*This day shall be a memorial feast for you....*

While the Bible contains other, more detailed descriptions of the Seder ritual at Passover (Leviticus 23:5–8; Numbers 9:2–5; Numbers 28:16ff; Deuteronomy 16:1–8), this one achieves special impact by virtue of its location in the biblical narrative. The Israelites are still in bondage. Nine plagues have been visited upon Egypt, and God has informed Moses of the tenth plague. The Seder almost certainly did not assume final shape until, at the earliest, the Jews' return to Palestine from Babylonian captivity, *circa* 520 B.C.E. We read this description where an editor has placed it, so that we might see it as a vital part of God's revelation to Moses. The ritual is to be seen as God's expectation, instituted as a part of the fight for freedom.

The Passover prayers are not listed here, but the familiar ceremonial foods are: roast lamb, unleavened bread, bitter herbs. All who partake must be dressed for flight. The blood of the lamb must mark Hebrew homes, for God will execute judgment on Egypt's inferior "gods" by striking all of Egypt's first-born children.

Modern sensibilities recoil from the notion of a bloodthirsty God slaying children to bend Egypt to the divine will. We should understand that the narrative describes a holy war conducted more than a millennium before Jesus' time, and that violence is a divine last resort. Here, God is warrior. Israel participates in the holy war not by committing violence, but by worshiping, celebrating the Seder.

### Responsorial Psalm: Psalm 116:12–13, 15–16, 17–18

### Second Reading: 1 Corinthians 11:23–26

*Do this in remembrance of me.*

This text presents what are often called the "words of institution" of the Eucharist. They are located in the middle of a section of the letter in which Paul tries to correct Corinthian abuses that have been brought to his attention. The entire eleventh chapter of the book deals with proper comportment at worship, with a focus on the divisions and attitudes that have corrupted Corinthian liturgies.

Here he describes the authentic tradition (literally, "that which is handed over"), in which the Lord's Supper is celebrated. Citing Jesus' own words, Paul urges the church to eat the bread and drink the cup. These are Christ's body and blood, consumed in remembrance of him, and that is why we worship. It is pointless, and in fact sinful, to gather without this single purpose, as the rest of the chapter illustrates. Paul gives shape to the doctrine that later becomes embedded in the accounts of the four evangelists.

### Gospel: John 13:1–15
*...as I have done, so you must do.*

This episode places Jesus and disciples at table *before* the feast of the Passover. Where other evangelists describe Jesus breaking bread (Matthew 26:26–29, Mark 14:22–25, Luke 22:15–20), John portrays him washing the feet of the disciples. Over Peter's objections, Jesus describes the work of the church: "If I washed your feet, I who am 'teacher' and 'Lord,' then you must do the same."

For John, the meal is synonymous with servanthood. This narrative of Jesus as servant at the Last Supper completes a theology of the Eucharist. We reenact Jesus' foot-washing at this Mass of the Lord's Supper to complete the formal renewal of priestly vows inaugurated at the Chrism Mass. We remove the consecrated species from the tabernacle and strip the altar of its garments to draw attention to the Eucharist. After John's example, we accentuate the meal by its removal. To participate in the Lord's Supper, we must not only cast aside our divisions and focus our entire selves upon Christ's body and blood; in common with our ordained leaders, we must also recommit ourselves to serve. To eat is to become servants.

### Questions for Reflection
•How do you respond to the image of God as warrior? What images do you prefer? What must you do to make room for all of the Bible's various descriptions of God?

•How do you approach the eucharistic table? What must you change? What kind of support do you need to make any necessary changes?

•How has Jesus been your servant? How do you serve others? How can you act more faithfully as servant?

# EASTER TRIDUUM
## GOOD FRIDAY:
## CELEBRATION OF THE LORD'S PASSION

### Dying

*[April 5, 1996; April 2, 1999; April 5, 2002]*

No Mass is permitted on this day. The service consists of three parts: a liturgy of the word, which includes lengthy intercessory prayers; Veneration of the cross; Communion, distributing species consecrated at Holy Thursday's Mass of the Lord's Supper.

### First Reading: Isaiah 52:13–53:12

*Yet it was our infirmities that he bore, our sufferings that he endured.*
This is the entire fourth song of God's servant, the work of "second Isaiah." From the earliest generations the church has recognized Jesus in these representative phrases: "... So marred was his look ... He was spurned and avoided ... A man of suffering, accustomed to infirmity ... We held him in no esteem ... Yet it was our sins he bore, our sufferings he endured ... He was pierced for our offenses, crushed for our sins ... Like a lamb to the slaughter ... A grave was assigned to him among the wicked ... Though he had done no wrong ... The will of the Lord shall be accomplished through him ... He shall take away the sins of many and win pardon for their offenses." This magnificent poetry expands the core of the Christian creed.

We may not suppose that, five centuries early, the author intended these words to apply specifically to Jesus of Nazareth. Still, it is appropriate that we use them on this day, for the author probably envisioned a future servant, a *messiah* ("anointed," literally "oily one") in whose suffering all would be redeemed.

### Responsorial Psalm: Psalm 31:2, 6, 12–13, 15–16, 17, 25

### Second Reading: Hebrews 4:14–16; 5:7–9

*...he learned obedience from what he suffered. ...*
These verses from the often-polemical letter to the Hebrews identify Jesus Christ as the servant described in the first reading. Christian doctrine is also stated explicitly: "Tempted in every way, he never

sinned; when perfected, he offered salvation to all who obey him; he learned obedience through suffering." Although no one wants to suffer, this text shows us the way to salvation. We learn obedience in suffering. Contrast this portrait with yesterday's Exodus picture of God as warrior.

## Gospel: John 18:1–19:42
*I am he....*

We can see John's literary and theological genius at work, as the passion begins and ends in a garden. The author echoes the Bible's account of human origins and purpose (Genesis 2:8) with this narrative device. In a similar manner, when apprehended by the crowd, Jesus asks "Whom do you seek?" echoing his own first words in this account of the gospel (1:38: "What do you seek?"). His arrest closes that chapter of his ministry in which he walks freely and summons followers. A new chapter begins, a story of suffering and death. Identifying himself explicitly with the Father, Jesus repeats the divine name that is not supposed to be uttered: "I am" (18:5; 18:8; see also Exodus 3:14).

The actions of the "other disciple" may be included as a foil of, and a contrast to, those of Peter. He follows Jesus to the end, while Peter abandons the Lord, even reversing God's name: "I am not!" (18:17; 18:25). Scholars argue that despite 21:24 this other disciple cannot have been the author. Any eyewitnesses were dead long before this gospel was composed.

Hauled in front of the authorities, Jesus turns the tables. He places them on trial. In Jesus' tribunal, Pilate is a sympathetic figure. He and Rome are exonerated. It is not his fault that he cannot recognize the one who is the Truth standing before him. By contrast, "the Jews" are seen to manipulate their own law to accomplish Jesus' demise before the festival of the Passover. Their hypocrisy lies exposed before the blameless Jesus. They have engineered Jesus' death and tied Pilate's hands. The only decision he can make is to express his contempt for this people he must govern by labeling the crucified Jesus "King of the Jews."

Catholic doctrine condemns explicitly any form of anti-Jewish invective (*Nostra Aetate*, 4; *Catechism of the Catholic Church*, 839). We must read John's ironies with this teaching in mind, and remember that the evangelist's purpose is not to blame, but to encourage faith. We must remember another irony: Peter, the first bishop of Rome, has played a role in Jesus' demise. This narrative asks us to recognize the One who is the Truth, and places us all on trial.

## Questions for Reflection

•How do you deal with suffering?

•When do your actions resemble those of Jesus' accusers? How does Jesus respond to you?

•Whom do you seek? What do you do when Jesus stands before you?

# EASTER TRIDUUM
## VIGIL

*Peace!*

*[April 6 or 7, 1996; April 3 or 4, 1999; April 6 or 7, 2002]*

The Easter Vigil as we know it was inaugurated by Pius XII in 1950. Its symbols and movements echo the devotions our ancestors celebrated as they vigiled through the three days and the nights of their Easter celebrations. Ancient practice often culminated in baptisms at dawn. Our restored catechumenate has reclaimed this dimension, as well.

The Vigil begins in darkness, the congregation assembled outside the sanctuary. A bonfire chases away the dark and the cold, and the Easter candle is presented, blessed, and lit. The congregation proceeds to the baptismal pool, where the readings proclaim many of our best stories.

### First Reading: Genesis 1:1–2:2
*In the beginning....*

In bold and economical strokes, the first of two creation stories narrates events of an unimaginably huge scale. In so doing, the story sets forth a distinct Hebrew cosmology, a "theory of everything."

In contrast to the cosmologies of other ancient peoples, here there are no divine skirmishes. In the beginning...God created the heavens and the earth, with word, not in battle. In a mere five days God commands into being light, arrangements of water and vegetation, the lights of the night sky, and creatures upon the earth. There are no battles, only God's will, and God's daily judgment that it is good. On the sixth day God creates the human person in the divine image, male and female. Now, before the sabbath rest, God says it is *very* good. Human beings are the climax of creation and, unique among creatures, were made in God's image.

### Responsorial Psalm:
### Psalm 104:1–2, 5–6, 10, 12, 13–14, 24, 35
### or Psalm 33:4–5, 6–7, 12–13, 20–22

### Second Reading: Genesis 22:1–18
*I will bless you abundantly....*

This is the climax of the cycle of Abraham stories, which occupy Genesis chapters 12–25. Over against God's promises of countless descendants (13:16; 16:10), Abraham learns that he must sacrifice his son, Isaac. It is an absurd and terrifying divine demand, which seems to frustrate not only God's covenant with Abraham, but also the purpose of creation.

This troublesome story narrates discernment and God's faithfulness. It is a contest between right faith and wrong faith. Most other gods demand human sacrifice (see 1 Kings 16:34, for example). Could Abraham's mysterious and magnificent God do any less? Abraham bundles the child off to Moriah, responding faithfully to God's request. As his blade begins its descent toward the child's neck, Abraham hears God's messenger: "Do not harm the boy!" Having let go of his most cherished hopes, Abraham learns God's will: God cherishes us.

### Responsorial Psalm: Psalm 16:5, 8, 9–10, 11

### Third Reading: Exodus 14:15–15:1
*...the Israelites marched into the midst of the sea on dry land.*

The exodus is the formative event in Hebrew history. In this liturgy as in the biblical canon, this rousing story is followed by the equally rousing Song of Miriam.

From beginning to end, God is in control. God makes pharaoh's heart obstinate, but at God's command Moses holds his hand over the sea, which parts for the chosen people. After Israel has passed through the sea safely, God directs Moses to stretch out his hands again, and the Egyptian army is destroyed.

The exodus is a passage from slavery into freedom, but also a passage from a stratified order into wilderness, from begrudging dependence into independence and hardship. A community liberated by God must now rely upon God for everything. Christ's passage from death to life echoes this saving event.

### Responsorial Psalm: Exodus 15:1–2, 3–4, 5–6, 17–18

### Fourth Reading: Isaiah 54:5–14
*The Lord calls you back.*

The chief image describes the relationship between God and the people: "Your creator is your husband. You are like a wife abandoned in the husband's moment of anger." The image is not attractive at face value, but consider that, unlike any human husband, the creator-spouse is always righteous. God has allowed the people to be exiled because they have been a wayward and unfaithful spouse. God has never stopped loving this people, and promises now never to rebuke them again.

This text comforts. "With great tenderness I will take you back.... My love shall never leave you.... Great shall be the peace of your children." God will not abandon the people, even if the natural order collapses. The climax is both promise and challenge: "You shall be established in justice." The people's past failures to do justice constituted the waywardness that an angry God punished with exile. Justice requires that they be restored to their home, but also that they become an ethical beacon for the rest of the world.

## Responsorial Psalm: Psalm 30:2, 4, 5–6, 11–12, 13

## Fifth Reading: Isaiah 55:1–11
*All you who are thirsty, come to the water!*

This reading climaxes "second Isaiah," but it does not include the chapter's final verses. God invites the audience to a meal at an oasis in the desert. "Do not waste your money on what cannot satisfy," says the prophet. "Listen to God's word, and you will eat well." The meal renews the everlasting covenant. Even so, God's people cannot only look inward, for they are to be a sign of God's saving presence in the world.

The poet speaks of repentance both personal and corporate. If the scoundrel forsakes his ways, he accepts responsibility for the poor and the marginated. God forgives generously. The gulf between God's ways and our ways is enormous, like the distance between the heavens and the earth.

God's word is like water that journeys through the world with a purpose, and that returns to the heavens only after it has met its purpose. God's word is alive, pervasive, both life-giving and destructive, not confined to human words, available and vital at all times. The omitted verses complete this picture of God's banquet as a commissioning: "You will leave here in joy, you will return in peace, and all creation will sing and dance for you; you will be a sign, this meal will be a sign; God's joy and peace will govern the earth, because of you." Perhaps the Vigil's sacraments embody these omitted verses.

### Responsorial Psalm: Isaiah 12:2–3, 4, 5–6

### Sixth Reading: Baruch 3:9–15, 32—4:4

*Such is our God: No other is to be compared to God.*

Baruch is one of the books included in Catholic Bibles but considered *apocryphal* (non-canonical) by Protestants and Jews. This text begins with the *Shema Israel*, the classic call to prayer, and it offers instruction to a people in exile. "You deserve your predicament," the prophet tells them, "because you have disobeyed God's wisdom." Some of the previous readings are summarized, in hopes that Israel will learn the commandments of life, but the text is not an iteration of Mosaic law. It is instead a transition from the law into something new, a reliance not upon laws written in books, but upon wisdom.

Wisdom is personified, feminine in gender. Many Catholic scholars find in the Jewish notion of wisdom the foundations of our doctrine of the Holy Spirit. She is the book of the precepts of God, a law that endures forever.

### Responsorial Psalm: Psalm 19:8, 9, 10, 11

### Seventh Reading: Ezekiel 36:16–28

*I will give you a new heart and place a new spirit within you.*

Here is a gloomy analysis of Israel's tenure in the promised land. The imagery is ugly: Their conduct was like the defilement of a menstruating woman. God acts, not for Israel's sake, but for God's own name, which Israel has profaned. God will restore this people and cleanse them in a ritual bath. God will replace their hearts of stone with natural hearts. God's spirit will dwell within them, and the evidence will be observed in their fidelity to divine statute. The promise is ancient and ever new: "You will be my people and I will be your God."

### Responsorial Psalm: Psalm 42:3, 5; 43:3, 4
### or Psalm 51:12–13, 14–15, 18–19

### Epistle: Romans 6:3–11

*...we too might live a new life.*

Paul interprets baptism. It is a burial with Christ, a burial that leads to new life. From now on, you are dead to sin, and alive through Jesus Christ.

**Responsorial Psalm: Psalm 118:1–2, 16, 17, 22–23**

## Gospel: Matthew 28:1–10
*Carry the good news....*

Mary Magdalene and "the other Mary" go to the tomb, where they witness an earthquake, an angel descending like lightning, and guards falling down as if dead. The angel urges them not to fear. Jesus has been raised, to fulfill his promise!

After they look into the empty tomb, the women run to announce the resurrection to the Twelve. *En route* they encounter Jesus, who greets them, "Peace. Do not fear." His greeting echoes and deepens the angel's announcement. The text dramatizes what happens when we encounter Jesus. The story leads the women through fear, to instruction and examination of evidence, and into faith. The evidence is set before us. We may be afraid, but we must examine the evidence at hand. And we are invited to believe.

After the homily, we enact these words. The congregation prays over the elect, asking them publicly to renounce Satan, to profess their faith, and to declare whether they come to the sacrament freely. One by one, these elect are baptized, clothed in white garments, and confirmed. They lead the congregation into the sanctuary, where, as neophytes, they will witness and participate in the Eucharist for the first time. They have become living examples of Christ risen before us, new evidence of his presence in the world.

## Questions for Reflection
• What do you fear? What aspects of our core saving event frighten you?

• What evidence shows you that Christ is risen?

• How will you receive Christ's gift of peace?

• How will you announce the resurrection?

# EASTER SUNDAY

## *He is risen*

*[April 7, 1996; April 4, 1999; April 7, 2002]*

### First Reading: Acts 10:34a, 37–43

*He commissioned us to preach to the people and to bear witness....*

Peter's audience in the home of the centurion Cornelius is just like us in one respect. We too have heard of Jesus' resurrection. But there is a big difference between hearing the story and becoming part of it.

Peter's sermon summarizes and interprets the gospel. Anointed with the Holy Spirit, Jesus did good works and healed. Executed, he was raised up on the third day. He has commissioned us to bear witness to him. Everyone who believes in him has forgiveness of sins.

Even though Peter's audience has heard the story, something is new. At the end of his talk, in verses not included here, the whole crowd receives the Holy Spirit. We are not told how this happens, but we do see the effect. All believe in Jesus, and all are baptized. Their lives changed, they are now part of the gospel.

We have heard the story of Jesus' resurrection countless times. Maybe we have become part of the story, or maybe we remain spectators. Maybe this time there is something new.

### Responsorial Psalm: Psalm 118:1–2, 16–17, 22–23

### Second Reading: Colossians 3:1–4

*Your life is hidden now with Christ in God.*

Christ's resurrection is no mere historical curiosity. We have been raised up with him. Easter marks our freedom from all forms of death and from all the lesser dead ends that clutter our lives. Today we celebrate our new life.

### or 1 Corinthians 5:6b–8

*Get rid of the old yeast.*

Paul describes our former lives as bread leavened with yeast. But since even a tiny bit of yeast affects the entire dough, we must get rid of it. We must let go of any corruption that allows us to cling to our former lives. We must instead live as unleavened bread. Having let go of wickedness and corruption, we may now live in sincerity and truth.

## Gospel: John 20:1–9

*...the stone had been moved away.*

In John's first resurrection story the truth is unwrapped slowly and carefully. First, Mary Magdalene arrives at the tomb in the dark and sees that the stone has been rolled away. She runs to summon Peter, who races to the tomb with an unnamed "other disciple." The other disciple outruns Peter, reaching the tomb first. Without entering, he peers inside and sees wrappings lying on the ground. When Peter arrives, he goes into the tomb, where he sees the wrappings and notices the headcloth rolled up in a place by itself. Then the other disciple enters, sees, and believes. In John's account, he is the first to believe.

The truth is unwrapped slowly, just as it is in our lives. Sometimes, we are frightened by evidence that points to the truth, and all we can do is to run to find someone else to help us. This is Mary's response, but notice that even though she does not understand, still she announces the good news. Sometimes, like the disciple who outruns Peter, we pause to contemplate what stands before us. At other times, we walk right into and are enveloped by the greatest of all mysteries. We explore matters in great depth, without ever receiving the gift of belief. Sometimes, the evidence is set before us, and we simply see and believe.

These ways in which the truth is unfolded suggest a vital role for the church, in Cornelius's first-century Roman home and for us today. A glance at the empty tomb may move us, but it may not give us understanding or faith. Entering the tomb is important, and yet it is also very difficult. Even Peter cannot enter alone, but must enter in the company of another. And the other disciple believes after the church invites him into the empty tomb. God alone gives faith. We must help one another, and others outside the church, to hear the story and to enter the tomb.

## Questions for Reflection

• When did you first hear the story of Jesus' resurrection? Who or what has invited you into the story? How have you responded? What is keeping you from becoming more a part of the story?

• How do you balance understanding and believing? What do you understand but not believe? What do you believe but not understand? How do you keep your balance?

• How do you invite others to hear the story of Jesus' resurrection? What more can you do?

# SECOND SUNDAY OF EASTER

*Believe*

[April 14, 1996; April 11, 1999; April 14, 2002]

### First Reading: Acts 2:42–47

*Those who believed shared all things in common.*

After Peter's flawed but effective Pentecost speech, many thousands of listeners believed in Jesus and were baptized. These verses offer us a glimpse at their newly Christian lives. Recognizing Luke's artful construction of the Acts of the Apostles, however, we might say more correctly that these verses present an idealized portrait of the life and growth of the early church. They may also suggest what our lives ought to be.

The Christian life places significant demands upon believers. Along with attending to the apostles' instructions, the church must live a communal life, break bread, and pray. Additional practices sound downright countercultural, then and now. Believers share all things in common. They sell all they own and divide the proceeds according to the needs of each person. In joy and sincerity they eat together, praise God, and incidentally earn the approval of any and all observers.

### Responsorial Psalm: Psalm 118:2–4, 13–15, 22–24

### Second Reading: 1 Peter 1:3–9

*There is cause for rejoicing here.*

This entire letter is a treatise on baptism. Appropriately, it provides all the second readings for the Sundays of Easter. The first half of today's text is a liturgical formula that was probably recited at many early baptisms. The remaining verses seem to be a direct address to neophytes. Today, as in the first century, these people are our most visible and most precious symbols of renewal. They embody the central truth of our faith. More than anyone, they have embarked on the Easter journey through death into new life. We must rejoice with them, and because of them.

## Gospel: John 20:19–31

*Peace be with you.*

John recounts the risen Jesus' appearance to the disciples as they cower behind locked doors. Jesus offers them a single gift, the Holy Spirit—the most valuable of all gifts. He also describes three aspects of this gift. First, he wishes peace upon them. Amid their fears and the bitterness that surely has followed their desertion of him, Jesus offers them peace. But this is a wish with a cost, for the second aspect of Jesus' gift is the disciples' responsibility to carry out Jesus' mission. He sends them, as the Father has sent him. The third aspect of this gift is the core of Christian mission. The disciples are given authority to forgive sins and hold sins bound, which in John's gospel is synonymous with discernment between belief and unbelief. They exercise this authority wisely and carefully, and never apart from the Holy Spirit. And most often they must forgive, for that is what they have learned from Jesus.

The second half of this text presents Thomas's doubts and his eventual recognition of Jesus. Having been absent, he insists that he will only believe when he can see Jesus and touch his wounds. Jesus appears one week later, and this time Thomas is present. Jesus echoes his earlier greeting of peace and the Holy Spirit, and invites Thomas to explore all the evidence. Thomas responds with the climax of John's account of the gospel: "My Lord and my God!" Jesus appears to rebuke him, but really he offers an invitation to us and to the whole world. Blessed, says Jesus, are the ones who have not seen as Thomas has seen, and who have yet believed.

## Questions for Reflection

•What do you do in joy and sincerity? How closely do these actions resemble the communal life, apostolic instruction, frequent worship, and social responsibility described in the first reading?

•How has Jesus equipped us to meet our responsibilities? What gifts has he given to us?

•What are the responsibilities of the church? In what ways do you contribute to the church meeting our shared responsibilities? How can you improve your contribution?

# THIRD SUNDAY OF EASTER

*Hearts burning within us*

[April 21, 1996; April 18, 1999; April 21, 2002]

### First Reading: Acts 2:14, 22–28
*God freed him from death's bitter pangs.*

Peter's long Pentecost sermon interprets three portions of the Hebrew Bible in a way that sees Christ as both point of reference and fulfillment of all previous tradition. It also establishes a pattern repeated throughout the Acts of the Apostles and echoed in ancient and modern liturgy. It lends official weight to a Christian way of reading Hebrew texts that finds predictions fulfilled by Jesus Christ.

This portion of the sermon cites Psalm 16 to suggest that Jesus of Nazareth is none other than the God who saved David from peril, time and time again. This interpretation is introduced by a thumbnail sketch of Jesus' life, career, death, and resurrection. Together, sketch and interpretation indict the listeners, while also offering hope and life.

In ordinary circumstances a speaker with this daring sort of message would be drawn and quartered. Here, instead, upon hearing Peter's words, some three thousand are baptized. It is not likely that this is an accurate historical report. The author has other concerns, however. He wants us to understand that only the Holy Spirit could make possible both Peter's speech and its reception, which seems even more spectacular than that which greeted any of Jesus' own teaching.

### Responsorial Psalm: Psalm 16:1–2, 5, 7–8, 9–10, 11

### Second Reading: 1 Peter 1:17–21
*It is through him you are believers in God.*

These verses from an ancient baptismal treatise suggest that the Christian is on a sojourn in a strange land. The life in which everything used to be familiar is gone now, erased by the Christian's baptismal journey into Christ's death and resurrection. Stranded in a strange place, the Christian can only find his or her way centered in God.

### Gospel: Luke 24:13–35
*Were not our hearts burning inside us?*

Luke's climactic story is set on the day of the resurrection. Two disciples leave Jerusalem for the seven mile walk to Emmaus. They have heard of the empty tomb, and now they may be fleeing. As they walk, a stranger joins them. When he asks about the topic of their conversation, they express surprise that he has not heard of the things that occurred recently in the city. When he asks for details, they sketch the contours of the gospel, which they know but do not yet believe: Jesus was a prophet powerful in word and deed, they say, who was executed by the authorities, and of whom the most astonishing thing has now been claimed. Some people insist that he is alive. These disciples know the whole story, but they are not yet part of it.

The stranger calls them some unflattering names: dense, slow, senseless. They have failed to believe what the prophets have announced. He interprets every passage in the holy books that refers to Jesus. At Emmaus, the two disciples invite the stranger to join them, and when he breaks bread they recognize him. He is Jesus, but now he has vanished from their sight. They race back to Jerusalem, where they join the other disciples and tell them about their encounter with the Lord.

This story works on many levels. At face value, of course, it narrates a resurrection appearance. It also describes different dynamics in prayer, as the disciples address, then listen to, and finally recognize, Jesus. In addition, it portrays the structure of the conversion journey that has given shape to ancient and modern catechumenates. It seems to describe a method of catechesis that announces the message but that also insists that learners participate in community, worship, and mission. Most of all, it reflects the shape of worship. We gather, we interpret the Word, we break bread, we depart to resume our missions in the world. And in all these things the Holy Spirit burns like a fire within us.

## Questions for Reflection

•How do you read the Bible? As you read, how much attention do you give to your overall impressions, especially as your Christian faith has shaped them; the text's literary devices, context, integrity, and various interpretations in history; points of view that collide, and sometimes conflict, with your own?

•In what ways does your faith make you a stranger sojourning in a strange land?

•Where are you on your round trip between Jerusalem and Emmaus? What evidence suggests that you are just getting started; somewhere along the way in Emmaus; returning or returned to Jerusalem; somewhere else? What help do you need to continue your journey?

# FOURTH SUNDAY OF EASTER

*The real shepherd*

*[April 28, 1996; April 25, 1999; April 28, 2002]*

### First Reading: Acts 2:14a, 36–41

*You must reform and be baptized.*

Hearing Peter's speech on what we now know as the first Christian Pentecost, many in the crowd are deeply shaken. Peter has interpreted portions of Hebrew tradition in terms of the most basic Christian beliefs: Christ has died. Christ has risen. Christ comes again through the Holy Spirit. The crowds ask Peter and the other disciples what they must do. Echoing the response of John the Baptizer (Luke 3:10), the answer describes the core of our Easter celebration: to reform, be baptized and forgiven, and receive the Holy Spirit.

We should not lose sight of the irony in Peter's sudden heroic stature. Luke's own timeline reminds us that, not long ago, on three separate occasions, Peter had denied even knowing Jesus (Luke 22:54–62). Now, just two months later, he is winning converts in heroic proportions. Maybe this irony is more instructive than the narrative itself. Having seen the depths to which Peter can sink, we can only marvel at whatever power sets him preaching before a huge crowd. It can only be the Holy Spirit.

### Responsorial Psalm: Psalm 23:1–3, 3–4, 5, 6

### Second Reading: 1 Peter 2:20b–25

*By his wounds you were healed.*

Here is the central irony in Christian belief: Jesus' death has given us life. In his own body he brought our sins to the cross, so that now, dead to sin, we can live in accord with God's will.

For the author of the baptismal homilies that constitute this letter, Christ is our example. When we follow in his footsteps we live according to God's will. Sometimes this means that we must suffer, refusing to cause suffering. Always, we must pattern our choices upon the irony that resides at the core of our lives.

### Gospel: John 10:1–10

*The sheep hear his voice.*

Immediately after giving sight to a man born blind, Jesus offers a cryptic teaching to an unspecified audience. If you climb into the sheepfold without using the gate, you are a thief and a marauder. If you enter through the gate, you are the shepherd. The sheep will follow the shepherd, not the stranger. In response to his audience's puzzlement, Jesus gets very specific. "I am the sheepgate," he says. "All of my predecessors were thieves and marauders. Whoever enters through the gate will find safety, freedom of movement, and pasture. While the thief comes to destroy, I came to give life to the full."

This is hard, uncompromising language that seems to manifest the poisonous relations that existed between Jews and Christians at the time when this gospel account was written. It may be a reflection upon the voluntary unbelief of those who have ejected from the synagogue the man born blind (9:34) and who have claimed to see, while failing to see the Christ (9:41). We modern Christians must do our best to recognize and overcome such enmity. We can begin to do this by focusing on the main point of these verses: Jesus offers fullness of life.

Underneath its apparent anti-Jewishness, this episode may have been included in John's account to challenge the motives, and perhaps the liturgical practices and beliefs, of people calling themselves Christians. It recasts in new terms, and for a new context, the classic biblical struggle between right faith and wrong faith. Those who believe wrongly follow the stranger, who is both thief and marauder. To believe rightly, we must follow the shepherd, the one who enters through the gate.

This text remains ever obscure. Even so, we can and should use these hard words to examine ourselves and our motives.

## Questions for Reflection

•What aspects of your life continue to need reform?

•Why is it appropriate that baptism provide a focus for our Easter celebration and reflection?

•How do you recognize the shepherd? What evidence tells you that you are following the shepherd? What evidence could suggest that you occasionally follow a thief?

# FIFTH SUNDAY OF EASTER

*Doing even greater things*

*[May 5, 1996; May 2, 1999; May 5, 2002]*

### First Reading: Acts 6:1–7

*The word of God continued to spread.*

Luke presents a highly stylized "history" in the Acts of the Apostles. We cannot read his descriptions of events as factually accurate reports of what happened. Luke's purpose is to use historical occurrences to instruct us in the ways of belief, and to invite us into faith.

Even so, occasionally we can glimpse at facts underlying the fast-paced narrative. These verses focus on a complaint of some Greek-speaking believers. Compared to the community's treatment of those who speak Hebrew, widows in the Greek-speaking portion of the community are neglected in the daily distribution of food. Clearly the linguistic miracle of Pentecost has not solved all problems. It is certain that conflicts of this sort arose early in the life of the church. Here we see a crisis: The community must live up to its egalitarian rhetoric.

Luke teaches that the Twelve resolve the problem by convening the entire community of disciples. The narrative hints at a meeting of thousands. This huge assembly must look for seven men known to be deeply spiritual and prudent, to be appointed to the task of distributing food. Seven are selected and presented to the apostles. The Twelve pray over them and impose hands on them. They are Stephen, Philip, Prochorus, Nicanor, Timon, Parmenas, and Nicolaus of Antioch. This latter man, a convert to Judaism, appears to have been among the first Gentile-born Christians.

This solution is at once functional and problematic. Now food will be distributed reliably. On the other hand, professional ministers have taken on some of the community's responsibilities. Moreover, the Twelve have become more than teachers. Now they have done some organizing. Through church history, tension is always evident between the community's duties and those of its leaders.

### Responsorial Psalm: Psalm 33:1–2, 4–5, 18–19

## Second Reading: 1 Peter 2:4–9
*You too are living stones.*

Citing several passages in the Jewish Scriptures, this baptismal treatise introduces the notion of a mighty structure built with "living stones." The cornerstone is Christ, who is also a stumbling-block for nonbelievers. We who are the baptized are invited to allow ourselves to be built "as an edifice of spirit, a holy priesthood." The author speaks of Christians in the phrase that the Hebrew people use to speak of the Jews. The author regards Christians as God's "chosen race," whose purpose is to proclaim God's works. We must read this text in light of modern Catholic teaching that recognizes that God has not revoked the covenant with the Jews (*Catechism of the Catholic Church* #839).

## Gospel: John 14:1–12
*I am the way, and the truth, and the life.*

At the Last Supper, after predicting Judas's betrayal and Peter's denials, Jesus consoles the eleven in advance of the disturbing events that will transpire soon. He offers his "last discourse" in the three chapters that conclude with his arrest and passion. The entire discourse is addressed to any audience of the faithful who already recognize Jesus as God incarnate. This text is part of the discourse, and it has three parts. First, Jesus insists that he goes before us to prepare a place for us in the Father's house. Next, in response to Thomas's question, Jesus states explicitly, "I am the way, the truth, and the life." Finally, he insists that to see him is to have seen the Father, and that anyone who has faith in him will do his work and even greater things.

This latter statement is both a promise and a challenge. It helps to explain why and how Peter can become the hero whose exploits are narrated in Acts. It also holds the disciples, including us, to a very high standard of action. We who follow the way, the truth, and the life must also show the way, do the truth, and live the life we proclaim.

## Questions for Reflection

•How is conflict handled in today's church, both locally and globally? How does contemporary practice compare or contrast with the episode described in the first reading?

•Who does the work of the church? Who should do the work of the church? What role do you play? What role do you think you ought to play? What changes must you make, if any?

•How does the church seem to do "even greater things"? How do you do "even greater things"?

# SIXTH SUNDAY OF EASTER

*One in the Spirit*

[May 12, 1996; May 9, 1999; May 12, 2002]

### First Reading: Acts 8:5–8, 14–17

*...they received the Holy Spirit.*

These verses hint at disagreements in the growing church concerning baptisms that Philip has celebrated. Following the appointment of seven men to distribute the community's food (see last Sunday's first reading), the Acts of the Apostles describes the exploits of two of them who have taken on additional responsibilities. Like the Twelve, they preach, and in some cases they baptize. Hauled in to face the Sanhedrin, Stephen has hurled accusations upon them and he has become the first Christian martyr (6:8–7:60). The second appointee, Philip, is far more fortunate, traveling and making converts.

Even so, he seems to have created some disagreements. His baptisms in Samaria are not considered complete by powerful factions in the church. Philip has baptized only in the name of the Lord Jesus. Peter and John go to Samaria later, to impose hands upon the baptized, so that they might receive the Holy Spirit.

Are we to view Philip as some renegade who was doing something outrageous? Maybe, but it is more likely that even through Luke's stylized history we can catch a glimpse of an early conflict among well-intentioned people, and the steps that seem to have been taken to deal with that conflict. We must remember that Luke's account of events is not a news report. It was written a half-century after the events, long after basic understandings of baptism, Gentile conversion, and myriad other issues had been worked out. To this point in the narrative, his account has not even mentioned the conversion of Paul. Yet throughout the adventure that is the Acts of the Apostles, Luke has taken Paul's theology for granted.

Luke's narrative shows us that the church baptizes in the name of the Father and of the Son and of the Spirit. It also suggests that this fundamental point of doctrine, as all doctrine, had to be thrashed out in practice, in conflict, and, most of all, in prayer.

### Responsorial Psalm: Psalm 66:1–3, 4–5, 6–7, 16, 20

### Second Reading: 1 Peter 3:15–18
*Keep your conscience clear.*
The baptism treatise continues: "Make your hearts into places where the Lord is worshiped. Speak gently and respectfully, and always answer anyone who wonders about your source of extraordinary hope and strength. Keep your conscience clear, so that no one can hold anything against you. Endure any suffering that comes your way as a result of your good deeds. Imitate Christ, the just one who suffered for the sake of the unjust."

### Gospel: John 14:15–21
*I will not leave you orphaned.*
Continuing the "last discourse," John portrays Jesús describing a Paraclete, the Spirit to be given to those of us who love Jesus and obey his commands. The Spirit will be with us always. The world will neither recognize nor accept the Spirit. We who love Jesus and obey his commands can recognize the Spirit.

The strange word *Paraclete* may be understood as "advocate" or "intercessor." The more important word in this text, however, is *another*. John intends us to see Jesus, too, as advocate-intercessor. The Holy Spirit, the "other paraclete," is to dwell within us, so that we may function in ways that resemble and continue Jesus' own work in the world.

In effect, this text is John's own expression of the church as the body of Christ (see Romans 12; 1 Corinthians 12). We in whom the Spirit dwells will do Jesus' work, and then some.

### Questions for Reflection
•Does it matter how we baptize? Why won't just any well-intentioned words do?

•What disagreements or misunderstandings do you see in the church today? How are such things handled at your parish? How are disagreements handled in the universal church?

•How do we know the Spirit dwells within us, that is, the church? What evidence suggests that we are fulfilling the promise made to us and on our behalf? What evidence suggests that we must improve?

# ASCENSION OF OUR LORD

*You will receive power*

[May 16, 1996; May 13, 1999; May 16, 2002]

### First Reading: Acts 1:1–11

*...within a few days you will be baptized with the Holy Spirit.*

Of all the evangelists, only Luke has given us two volumes. Here in the opening verses of the Acts of the Apostles, he makes the transition from his account of the gospel to its sequel. Like the first book, this is addressed to Theophilus, literally "one who loves God." It is unknown, and immaterial, whether this Theophilus ever existed historically. After the greeting, Luke summarizes the first book, which deals with all that Jesus did and taught until he was taken up. He who had died appeared to his apostles many times during forty days to teach them about the kingdom of God. And he directed them to remain in Jerusalem until their baptism in the Holy Spirit.

Next Luke narrates the ascension a second time. The apostles ask Jesus, "Are you going to restore the kingdom to Israel now?" and he redirects their attention. He teaches them that they will receive power when the Holy Spirit descends, and that they will bear witness to him throughout the earth. With that, Jesus is lifted up from their sight.

The story concludes with two men dressed in dazzling garments posing a question to the apostles: "Why do you stand here looking up at the skies? Jesus will return." Their appearance parallels exactly the appearance of two men who soften the terror of the women who discover the empty tomb (Luke 24:4–7). They, too, ask a question: "Why do you seek the living one among the dead?"

These messengers speak matter-of-factly, as if to say, "This is just what happens when God acts in our lives." In both encounters, the witnesses have been changed, and now they have work to do. Here, the two men in dazzling clothes underline what Jesus has already taught: "You will receive the Spirit. You will announce the good news to the world." Because they remind us explicitly of the messengers at the empty tomb, they also establish the purpose of this book. The ascension interprets the resurrection, just as the men at the tomb have done. It offers the beginning of Luke's long answer to the question, Who reveals the presence of the risen Christ in the world?

## Second Reading: Ephesians 1:17–23

*God has put all things under Christ's feet.*

These verses show implicit knowledge of Christ's ascension: "…and seating him at his right hand in heaven." The same sort of knowledge appears in our creed. Clearly, Christ's ascension became an important doctrine early in the life of the church. The author prays for an enlightening spirit of wisdom and insight for the converted pagans of Ephesus, for their recognition of the enormous power of God who has raised Jesus from the dead. The image of Christ's body is used to describe the church in rich terms. The church is the fullness of the one who fills the universe. It may be that this statement is a wish for what might be, rather than a statement of fact. If so, it holds us responsible to make things happen.

## Gospel: Matthew 28:16–20

*Baptize them in the name of the Father and of the Son and of the Holy Spirit.*

Matthew's account of the gospel does not narrate an ascension in the manner of Luke. It does, however, portray Jesus' "farewell address." These concluding verses evoke a scene similar to that of the sermon on the mount (5:1), which in its own turn echoes Moses' gift of the law to the people of Israel at the entry to the promised land (Deuteronomy 1:1–5ff). It is a challenging farewell. In the place of laws or beatitudes, Jesus makes a simple directive: "Go, make disciples of all. Baptize them in the name of the Father and of the Son and of the Holy Spirit, and teach them to observe everything I have commanded." And the farewell ends on a promise: "I am always with you."

Although an ascension is not narrated, Matthew wants us to understand that Jesus is no longer visible as he is portrayed in these verses. Even so, he remains present in the church. He will be present always, until the end of the world.

## Questions for Reflection

•Who reveals the presence of Christ in the world? What evidence supports your answer or answers?

•How well is the church fulfilling the task that Jesus has set for us? If we must, how can we improve? What are you willing to do to help with this improvement?

•Why does Jesus assure us that he is always with us? Why is it important that we know this?

# SEVENTH SUNDAY OF EASTER

## *Glory*

*[May 19, 1996; May 16, 1999; May 19, 2002]*

### First Reading: Acts 1:12–14

*...they devoted themselves to constant prayer.*

After Jesus' ascension, and before receiving the Spirit, the apostles and the others who constitute the tiny church seclude themselves to pray constantly. This episode describes a calm amid the great and spectacular events of Easter. The church huddles together. By now they know that their fates are utterly in Christ's hands.

We should notice, too, that in contrast with synagogue practice of the time, women are included. Luke has narrated the beginnings of the church's institutional break from Jewish practice, without drawing attention to it. This neither-male-nor-female Christian habit is stated matter-of-factly, as if any controversy has long since been handled. For Luke, this is the way things are, the way they are supposed to be.

As they huddle, Jesus' followers cannot really know what lies in store for them. By now they know that Jesus keeps all of his promises, and that somehow, therefore, they will receive power. Whether each Christian trusts God completely at this point we cannot say. Luke's snapshot shows us, however, that they have no other choice.

### Responsorial Psalm: Psalm 27:1, 4, 7–8

### Second Reading: 1 Peter 4:13–16

*Rejoice, insofar as you share Christ's sufferings.*

This text repeats themes developed earlier. The Christian might have to suffer, and he or she must do so cheerfully, after Christ's example. God's glory is revealed in the suffering of every disciple, if that suffering is due to just causes. There is no glory in suffering when it results from our own sins, like murder, theft, or violating another's rights.

A treatise consisting of teaching given to the newly baptized, 1 Peter is a challenging handbook showing how Christians can function in a world that tends to reward corruption. These verses set the foundation for Catholic moral thought, in which an informed conscience is the best guide to authentically Christian choices and behavior. Some things are absolutely, objectively wrong, and we must avoid them. We must also examine the ways in which our actions affect others, to determine the purity of our behavior. This text clearly reflects persecutions suffered by early Christians. In a very different context it also speaks to us.

## Gospel: John 17:1–11a
*It is in them that I have been glorified.*

Of the four canonical gospels, John's is the newest and the most like classical Greek drama. Its prologue reminds us of a Greek chorus, which tells the basic shape of the drama in advance. Such a device may tend to diminish suspense, but it also enables John, more than the other evangelists, to cast Jesus explicitly as resurrected and divine teacher. The tone of the entire work shows that Jesus has been resurrected. Historical sequence is of minimal importance.

The "last discourse," which occupies chapters 14 through 17, is set between the last supper and Jesus' arrest. But because historical sequence is relatively unimportant here, the discourse portrays Jesus as "mystagogue," as teacher interpreting reality through the lens of the resurrection.

In these verses, Jesus prays to the Father. Jesus is both priest and sacrifice. Like all priests before him and since, he asks God to look with favor upon the sacrifice to be performed. Like all sacrifices, this one is meant to reveal God's glory. But Jesus is the sacrifice as well as the priest. Unlike any other "god," Jesus' Father is not glorified in earthly power. The glory of this God is revealed in obedience, in service, and in a message of love, forgiveness, and peace.

Much of Jesus' prayer focuses on the apostles, whom the Father has entrusted to Jesus. As he prepares to depart the world, Jesus states the real significance of his sacrifice. As he has glorified God, so do the disciples glorify him. They remain in the world, empowered by the Spirit, who is a permanent and ongoing revelation of God's glory.

## Questions for Reflection

•How do you pray? How do you pray when you are alone, and how do you pray with others? What signs tell you that Jesus is present when you pray? How do you deal with the occasional sense of Jesus' absence?

•What does the word "glory" connote for you? How do John's ideas about God's glory compare or contrast with yours?

•How well do you obey? How enthusiastically do you serve, love, and forgive? What do you do to build peace?

# PENTECOST

## The spirit prompted them

*[May 26, 1996; May 23, 1999; May 26, 2002]*

### First Reading: Acts 2:1–11

*...each of us hears them speaking...about the marvels God has accomplished.*
Talk of the Holy Spirit is risky. Too often it can sound smug, justifying quirky individual behavior or an institution's unwillingness to change. But it is an essential part of our belief that the Spirit does grace our world, and prompts us to build peace, justice, and love, after Jesus' example. Christians recognized long ago that without the Spirit we can do nothing.

Fifty days after the Passover, on the day of Pentecost, Jews from all nations have made the pilgrimage to Jerusalem. Amid the noise of a great crowd, they hear a noise like a strong, driving wind. Soon after this, they witness something strange. Some Galileans speak, and everyone can understand. To the persons in the crowd the marvel is that each hears Peter and companions speaking in his and her native tongue.

Luke casts this event as the first public act of the church after Jesus' ascension. He gives us a glimpse into the room where the disciples hide. When they hear the noise, tongues like fire rest on each of them. They are filled with the Holy Spirit. They express themselves in foreign tongues and make bold proclamation. The marvel is that Peter, John, James, and the others go public just a few weeks after Jesus' execution. They have seen Jesus risen from the dead, but they also know that they are in peril. The real marvel is that the same bunch who had once deserted Jesus now burst upon a multinational assortment of people to announce Jesus' own good news.

### Responsorial Psalm: Psalm 104:1, 24, 29–30, 31, 34

### Second Reading: 1 Corinthians 12:3–7, 12–13

*There are different gifts but the same Spirit.*
The first verse seems to suggest that a person's ability to say particular words is evidence that the Holy Spirit has inspired him or her. But anyone can speak words. History offers countless examples of proper

words used improperly, and Jesus seems to have insisted consistently that words alone mean nothing.

To Paul, one says "Jesus is Lord" in words *and* in actions. Faithful actions have everything to do with Paul's understanding of unity-in-diversity. Most of the twelfth chapter of 1 Corinthians compares the various gifts in the church to the functions of different parts of the body. This text excerpts a few verses to represent the whole.

There are many gifts, but the same Spirit. We do different things, but for the same purpose, for the common good. There are many members in the body. We were all baptized in the one Spirit into the body that is Christ. Paul implies that when we use our gifts for the common good, we say with every fiber of our being, "Jesus is Lord." We can only do such a thing in the Holy Spirit.

### Gospel: John 20:19–23
*Receive the Holy Spirit.*

In one episode, Jesus fulfills the things he has predicted and interpreted in advance. In his last discourse he promised a peace that the world cannot give, and the constant assistance of the Holy Spirit. Here, appearing to the Twelve for the first time after his resurrection, he gives them peace and the Holy Spirit.

He also gives two things that were not foretold. Now that the church has received the Spirit, he can teach things that had not been accessible before. Jesus gives the church a job: "As the Father has sent me, so I send you." He also gives a grave authority, that of forgiving sins or of holding them bound. Keeping in mind that for John sin is virtually synonymous with unbelief, we may understand that our job is to invite the world into faith. We do this on the day of Pentecost and always through credible word and action. We could not do anything, except in the Holy Spirit.

## Questions for Reflection

•What signs convince you that the Holy Spirit acts in the world? What are some other signs that convince others of the Spirit's action?

•What are your most significant gifts? How do you use them for the common good? How might you use them more effectively?

•What is the church's job, in your own words? How do you contribute to this job? How can you make a better and more lasting contribution?

# TRINITY SUNDAY
## (SUNDAY AFTER PENTECOST)
### Father, Son, and Spirit
*[June 2, 1996; May 30, 1999; June 2, 2002]*

The first two Sundays after Pentecost and the Friday after the second Sunday are sometimes called "doctrinal feasts" because these and other such feasts celebrate truths that have been revealed to the church after the last word of the Bible was written. The doctrine of the Trinity, for example, certainly pervades the New Testament, but there is no explicit statement of this doctrine anywhere in the Bible. After the church had had time to study the Scriptures and to reflect upon its life in history, ecumenical councils in the second, third, and fourth centuries clarified this pivotal Catholic teaching. By contrast, biblical narrative supports directly our feasts of Easter, Pentecost, Christmas, and many others. Since the feast of the Trinity celebrates a doctrine of the church, it is called a "doctrinal feast."

But we must not assume that other feasts are not also doctrinal. All doctrine is born of reflection upon the biblical witness, as well as upon the church's ever-changing experience in history. In a broad sense, each time the church gathers to reflect upon biblical texts, and especially to celebrate the Eucharist, we celebrate a feast in which doctrine plays a major role.

### First Reading: Exodus 34:4–6, 8–9
*I am a merciful and gracious God.*

All of today's readings seem to answer the question "Who is God?" In the Exodus text Moses stands before a cloud from which God's voice emerges: "I am merciful, gracious, slow to anger and rich in kindness and fidelity." Admitting that his is a "stiff-necked" people, Moses begs this merciful God to travel with them in the desert, to pardon their sins, and to "receive us as your own." Here Moses learns that God, though a powerful, fearsome warrior-God, is also gentle and compassionate.

### Responsorial Psalm: Daniel 3:52, 53, 54, 55, 56

---

## Second Reading: 2 Corinthians 13:11–13

*Live in harmony and peace.*

Although the doctrine of the Trinity is not stated explicitly in the Bible, sometimes Paul speaks as though everyone already knows that God is Father, Son, and Holy Spirit. Here, at the end of the second letter to Corinth, he offers a blessing that suggests that already many Christians accept this teaching. Jesus Christ gives grace, the Father gives love, and the Holy Spirit binds us in *koinonia*, the "fellowship" of Christians, or better yet, the common life shared by members of the same body.

## Gospel: John 3:16–18

*God so loved the world....*

Why has God sent Jesus into the world? While this text portrays the very real possibility of condemnation, God's purpose is much more gentle. Jesus is the paramount expression of God's love for the world, of God's universal offer of eternal life. The Christian doctrine of the Trinity places God's love for us at the core of creation, salvation, and our ongoing life and work in the world. It also suggests ways that the persons of the Trinity relate with one another, and it portrays their distinct contributions to the world in which we live.

The chapter and verse references for the opening line of this text are often painted large and displayed at sporting events, especially televised ones. How often have you seen someone in the stands holding a banner that says "John 3:16"? The aggressive manner in which the verse is thrust into popular consciousness seems to warn viewers that God punishes. Especially in light of Exodus 34, which on this doctrinal occasion accompanies John 3:16, we must see God's anger as a last resort. God loves us and invites us to respond to the gift of divine love.

## Questions for Reflection

•How do you describe God? How well do the first reading's descriptions express what you believe? In addition to "merciful, gracious, slow to anger, rich in kindness and fidelity," who is God? What other words, phrases, or stories can you use to describe God?

•In what ways have you experienced God as Father? When has God touched you as your equal, as brother or sister? How often do you live in *koinonia*, the fellowship of the Holy Spirit that binds you with others in a common life?

•In what ways does the doctrine of the Trinity challenge you? What difficulties does it pose for you? How does this doctrine invite you to make changes in your way of doing things?

# CORPUS CHRISTI
## (BODY AND BLOOD OF CHRIST)
### *Eucharistic responsibility*

*[June 9, 1996; June 6, 1999; June 9, 2002]*

The Easter season is accomplished, and we celebrate three doctrinal feasts. The first is Trinity Sunday, which focuses on the most basic Christian teaching. On this, the second Sunday after Pentecost, our celebration accentuates the Eucharist. And Friday, following the second Sunday after Pentecost, is the solemnity of the Sacred Heart of Jesus, a devotion to Christ's humanity.

For the rest of the church year, we dwell in "ordinary time." These three doctrinal feasts remind us of the most important resources we have to sustain us through the year. Jesus has become one of us. He who is both God and human promises our salvation and sustains us with his body and blood through the Spirit of himself and the Father.

### First Reading: Deuteronomy 8:2–3, 14–18
*Not by bread alone do you live.*

This text is part of the second homily that Moses delivers to the people who stand poised at the entrance to the promised land. He reminds the people that manna was not the only gift that God gave them during their wanderings. More important, in fact, was the hunger that God also caused. This hunger showed the people their utter dependence upon God.

Bread is a sustaining food. For Moses' audience, bread means much more. Any ritual use of bread is a reminder of slavery and deliverance, of desert and survival, of hungers, thirsts, and satisfaction. And after the example of the exodus generation, we live by the most powerful of life-giving forces, by every word that comes forth from the mouth of the Lord.

### Responsorial Psalm: Psalm 147:12–13, 14–15, 19–20

### Second Reading: 1 Corinthians 10:16–17
*We all partake of the one loaf.*

This brief but powerful text contains two rhetorical questions: Is not the liturgical cup a sharing in the blood of Christ? Is not the bread a sharing in Christ's body? These questions are Paul's dramatic way of stating what he thinks is obvious, and what ought to be obvious to us. He also reminds us that we are made one when we partake together. Along with our Catholic faith's explicit assertion that bread and wine become body and blood, these statements comprise our eucharistic theology.

As Paul states the focal point of this feast, he reminds us of our responsibilities. When we partake in the Eucharist we share in the body and the blood of Christ.

## Gospel: John 6:51–58
*I myself am the living bread.*

This text comes from a long chapter describing a miraculous feeding and the many teachings and controversies that follow. Overall, John's sixth chapter reflects the Bible's most mature example of eucharistic theology. It is still not as explicit as later doctrinal formulations, but it is quite sophisticated. The harsh and uncompromising tone of these verses is unfortunate. It may reflect the evangelist's concern to repudiate controversies and heresies that arose in the late first century.

First, Jesus states explicitly that he is the living bread. His flesh is given for the life of the world. Then, when some listeners wonder about this, he intensifies his rhetoric. He insists that we must feed on his flesh and drink his blood for the sake of eternal life.

In a similar manner, Catholic belief permits no compromise. We eat Jesus' body and drink his blood. This is Eucharist.

## Questions for Reflection

•How did God sustain our ancestors in the desert? What are the many gifts through which God delivered the chosen people? How does God sustain us today? What are the gifts through which God promises to save us? Which gifts are harder to recognize than others?

•What are your most honest answers to the two questions that Paul poses in the second reading? In what ways do you continue to struggle with these crucial beliefs? What issues have been resolved for you, as you have struggled through the years?

•What responsibilities do we accept when we partake of Christ's body and blood? How well do you meet your responsibilities? How effectively does the entire church live up to our shared responsibilities? How can you help the church to become more effective?

# SECOND SUNDAY IN ORDINARY TIME

*Recognizing Jesus*

*[January 14, 1996; January 17, 1999; January 20, 2002]*

### First Reading: Isaiah 49:3, 5–6

*I will make you a light to the nations.*

The anonymous poet known as "second Isaiah" describes the mission of the servant of the Lord. At the moment of conception God has called the servant to lead the people of Israel back from captivity. But it is also the servant's purpose to be a light to the nations so that salvation may reach to the ends of the earth.

The prophet's first audience identified the servant in two ways. First, the servant is a divine figure who is yet to come, the *messiah*, who is expected to usher in the salvation of the world. But the servant is also the people themselves, a people responsible for shining a light before the nations by their righteous and just example.

We claim a share in that responsibility. What happens in the world is supposed to matter to us. To be "good Christians" is to engage ourselves in the sometimes messy work of bearing the good news of salvation in our most intimate relationships and everywhere in the world.

### Responsorial Psalm: Psalm 40:2, 4, 7–8, 8–9, 10

### Second Reading: 1 Corinthians 1:1–3

*Grace and peace from God our Father....*

Paul's first letter to the Corinthians offers us a detailed and complete expression of his mature theology. When we explore it we are examining the theological foundations of most of the New Testament, particularly of Matthew's, Mark's, and Luke's accounts of the gospel. This letter also introduces the earliest and most authoritative convictions of the first Christians.

In today's verses Paul greets his audience, as he does in most of his letters. He identifies himself as apostle, names the audience in terms of their calling to holiness, and expands his address to all who call on the name of Jesus. Finally he offers grace and peace.

## Gospel: John 1:29–34

*This is God's chosen One.*

The Gospel of John introduces Jesus with high drama, through a prologue that reminds us of a Greek chorus or an operatic overture (1:1–18). In the opening scene that follows, John the Baptizer commands the audience's attention with his call to repentance. The scene is busy and bright, and dominated by the Baptizer.

Enter Jesus. John recognizes him and drops everything to place Jesus at center stage. "This is the Lamb of God," he says. "He is the one foretold by the prophets, the one for whom I have prepared the way." For the Baptizer and the evangelist, Jesus is the servant described in today's first reading. The Baptizer offers this explanation of events: "I did not recognize him before, but now I do. The one who sent me has allowed me to recognize Jesus. He will baptize with the Holy Spirit." With this emphasis on *recognizing* Jesus, the Baptizer and the evangelist introduce a *motif* that is very important in this account of the gospel. To recognize Jesus is to believe and to act upon that belief. To see Jesus is to believe and to live.

With all of the gospel's emphasis on seeing/recognition, the testimony of a reliable witness is crucial. We begin "ordinary time" with the assurance of a most reliable witness that Jesus is God's chosen One. The Baptizer is portrayed as a summary of the prophets, and yet his role is that of messenger. He sees the Lamb of God and invites us to recognize him.

## Questions for Reflection

•How easy is it for you to think of yourself as God's servant? What things sometimes make it difficult for you to think and act as a servant?

•How do you recognize Jesus? What conditions help you to see him in our world? Who helps direct your sight to him?

•What things sometimes prevent you from seeing Jesus? How do you deal with those things?

•To see Jesus is to believe and to act on that belief. What difference does your faith make? How do you act on your belief?

# THIRD SUNDAY IN ORDINARY TIME

## Jesus calls

*[January 21, 1996; January 24, 1999; January 27, 2002]*

### First Reading: Isaiah 8:23–9:3

*The people who walked in darkness have seen a great light.*

Some of these verses are echoed in G. F. Handel's oratorio *Messiah*: "The people who walked in darkness have seen a great light; you have smashed the rod of their taskmaster." Isaiah gives us powerful images in which darkness is dispelled, gloom is overcome by joy, and a captive people is set free.

For our present purposes, however, the most important verse in this text may be the first: "He degraded the land of Zebulun and the land of Naphtali; but...he has glorified...the land west of the Jordan, the District of the Gentiles." This apparent geographic trivia is important because the gospel text for this day locates Jesus' activity in the same territory.

### Responsorial Psalm: Psalm 27:1, 4, 13–14

### Second Reading: 1 Corinthians 1:10–13, 17

*Be united in mind and judgment.*

Writing to the complex and contentious church at Corinth, Paul responds to distressing news. There are many factions within the church, and this situation is a scandal. Paul poses questions. "Has Christ been divided? Was anyone other than Christ crucified for you? Were you baptized in Paul's name?" Of course, the answer to each of these questions is "No." Therefore, Christians must be united in mind and judgment. The concluding verse reminds the audience of Paul's sole purpose. He does not baptize, but he preaches the gospel.

The contemporary relevance of this text seems obvious. In every parish, in every town, and throughout the world, Christians continue to act as though Christ is divided. We live the scandal of a fractured Christianity, and not only in the form of the many denominations that call themselves churches. Even among Catholics there are great global divisions and petty local disagreements. Parishioners too often squabble over issues of little consequence.

All these scandalous factions obscure the single message that resides at the core of our lives. Christ has been crucified to save us all. We live a scandal, and yet, like the church of Corinth, we profess a creed of union, especially in our eucharistic banquet. This text challenges us as it challenged its first audience. We must live according to the belief we profess.

### Gospel: Matthew 4:12–23
*The kingdom of heaven is at hand.*

Through ordinary time in year A, we read Matthew's account of the gospel. Beginning today and in the weeks ahead we read stories from Matthew in a sequence that more or less follows the order of the evangelist's narrative. We interrupt this sequence during the seasons of Lent and Easter and for occasional feast days. In addition, we omit some of the episodes in Matthew's account. Thus we read "semi-continuously."

In this episode, Jesus has been baptized and has fended off Satan in the desert. Now he hears of the arrest of John the Baptizer, and he withdraws to Capernaum, near Zebulun and Naphtali. For Matthew this action fulfills the verses of Isaiah that constitute today's first reading, as Jesus glorifies the territory west of the Jordan.

At this point in the narrative Jesus takes over where John has been forced to leave off, but with something new. Echoing the Baptizer's call to reform, he also insists that the kingdom of heaven is at hand. He calls as disciples Simon, Andrew, James, and John, all fishermen who abandon their nets to follow Jesus. They walk away from their livelihoods to become, in Jesus' words, fishers of men and women. Touring all of Galilee, Jesus glorifies that territory by teaching, proclaiming the good news, and healing the sick.

### Questions for Reflection

•How does God cast a great light onto our world? What evidence tells you that a people who walked in darkness have seen a great light? What evidence might lead you to make a different judgment?

•What role does the church play in revealing God's great light to the world? How do you or can you contribute to the church's role?

•How do you experience the scandal of a divided Christianity? What can you do to change things for the better?

•How does Jesus call you? What does Jesus call you to do? How do you meet his challenge to be a fisher of men and women?

# FOURTH SUNDAY IN ORDINARY TIME

*Blessed are you*

*[January 28, 1996; January 31, 1999; February 3, 2002]*

### First Reading: Zephaniah 2:3; 3:12–13
*Seek justice, seek humility.*

The short and not-very-sweet book of Zephaniah introduces the idea of the "remnant," that portion of the chosen people who have survived their ups and downs to bear witness to God's continuing presence in human affairs. At the author's moment in history, the northern kingdom of Israel has fallen, and its ten tribes have been dispersed, never to appear again. In the still-independent southern kingdom of Judah, various kings have corrupted Hebrew religion in their eagerness to please their Assyrian overlords. The once-fearsome Assyrian war machine has weakened, Egypt is menacing, and the resulting contest between empires has placed tiny Judah in peril.

Zephaniah predicts doom at the hands of an angry God, but he also describes a remnant. For their lack of faith the people will fall into ruin. Even so, "If you are humble and seek justice you may be spared God's wrath. You may be part of the remnant that will survive." The disasters to come will purify and restore what is most true in the Hebrew tradition: humility, justice, truthfulness, and righteousness in God's name.

Humility, justice, truthfulness, and righteousness are social virtues, not private ones. To do justice, we must act in the world and on behalf of everyone in the world. To live righteously we must do more than obey rules. We must also safeguard the rights and welfare of all persons, and of all creation. Only by living for others can the remnant thrive in humility and in truth.

### Responsorial Psalm: Psalm 146:6–7, 8–9, 9–10

### Second Reading: 1 Corinthians 1:26–31
*Not many of you are wise.*

Paul introduces a paradox that is close to the center of the gospel. Those whom God has chosen are rarely wise, influential, or well-born, as these terms are commonly understood. With these verses Paul continues to address the scandal of divisions and disputes among the

Christians in Corinth. More than this, however, Paul establishes a pattern describing the gospel in our lives. Christ fills empty vessels. We must empty ourselves, so that Christ may fill us. We must let go of our attachments to influence and status, and to what the world calls wisdom. Having let go of these things, we can receive Christ.

## Gospel: Matthew 5:1–12

*Be glad and rejoice, for your reward in heaven is great.*

Familiarity is not always a good thing. There is probably no portion of Jesus' teaching that is recognized more easily than the beatitudes, but how well do we know them? How well have we taken them into ourselves? How accurately do they describe our daily conduct?

At face value the beatitudes might seem to say that the world's poor should be grateful for what little they have and console themselves with a reward to come after death. Jesus seems to tell us that our time on earth is only some kind of trial, and that suffering is a good thing, in and of itself.

We can only draw these conclusions, however, if we hear the beatitudes selectively and narrowly, and therefore dishonestly. If we read these verses carefully, we find a different message. There is room for everyone in Jesus' list of the "blessed." Our economic and social standing are trivial matters. What really count are our motives. The beatitudes guide our choices, desires, goals, and dreams—in short, the things we want and the ways in which we go about getting what we want. We must also remember that the core of Jesus' teaching is his announcement that the kingdom is at hand; it is not a far-off place. Our motives matter above all. We must make peace and show mercy. We must live in humility and truth, in justice and righteousness, for the kingdom *is* at hand.

## Questions for Reflection

•What do you do to live in justice? How does this divine demand guide your choices and your actions? What improvements can you make?

•What kinds of things fill you up? How do you like Paul's insistence that you empty yourself so that Christ can fill you? How will you empty yourself?

•What do you want? Deep down inside, what motivates you?

•What evidence tells you that you are "blessed"?

•What difference does it make to you that the kingdom is at hand? How does this truth guide you?

# FIFTH SUNDAY IN ORDINARY TIME

*Salt and light*

*[February 4, 1996; February 7, 1999; February 10, 2002]*

### First Reading: Isaiah 58:7–10
*Share your bread with the hungry.*

Here is a straightforward description of obligation and promise. It is a charter for the Jewish people, who are, at the author's time, newly returned to their homeland from their exile in Babylon. We may read these verses as a charter for ourselves as well.

God wants us to feed the hungry, to shelter the oppressed and the homeless, to clothe the naked, to assist everyone who is needy. If we meet our responsibilities, our light will shine, our wounds will be healed, and we will be embraced in God's glory. God rewards our fidelity, which we express most perfectly in justice.

### Responsorial Psalm: Psalm 112:4–5, 6–7, 8–9

### Second Reading: 1 Corinthians 2:1–5
*Your faith rests...on the power of God.*

Paul draws attention to his own limitations, as contrasted with the eloquence of other Christian preachers. Yet he also makes a claim that sounds almost arrogant: "I speak of nothing but Jesus Christ, and because of this your faith rests upon the power of God." He tempers this apparent arrogance, however, by underlining his own weaknesses. He reminds the church at Corinth that when he had first come there he was afraid and insecure. Therefore, any good done through him was clearly God's accomplishment.

### Gospel: Matthew 5:13–16
*You are the salt of the earth.... You are the light of the world.*

The sermon on the mount occupies chapters five through seven in Matthew's account of the gospel. After opening with the beatitudes, Jesus continues with descriptions of two commonplace objects. Both describe the role of his disciples. The first object is salt, which is only worthwhile if it keeps its flavor. Perhaps this is a caution for the disciple: Never lose touch with essentials. The second object, light, is given more attention. As it would be foolish to hide a candle under a bushel basket, it would be foolish for the disciple to hide his or her light. The disciple must "shine before people," and thus lead them toward God. These images serve as a transition between the beatitudes and Jesus' interpretations of some of the commandments. The beatitudes are warm, welcoming, inviting. They create room for everyone, and they invite all into "blessing." The remainder of the sermon on the mount is demanding, as Jesus insists that the commandments must be obeyed in motive and intent, as well as in behavior. Matthew has set the images of salt and light between beatitudes and commandments to insist that the disciple must aspire to the highest ethical standards while always serving others. The Christian's essential nature is bound up with his or her service of others. As Paul reminds us, this is never a reason for bragging, but a defining principle under which we must live.

### Questions for Reflection

•What must you do in order to remain true to your essential nature? How deeply does your faith define you? In practice, how close is your Christian faith to your essential nature?

•How do you feed the hungry? How do your actions help to shelter the oppressed and the homeless, clothe the naked, assist the needy?

•How can you improve your response to the divine charter set before the chosen people, and before you as well?

# SIXTH SUNDAY IN ORDINARY TIME

*Holiness*

*[February 11, 1996; February 14, 1999; February 17, 2002]*

### First Reading: Sirach 15:15–20
*It is loyalty to do God's will.*

Seven books, and fragments of two books, are considered part of the
Bible by Catholics alone. Protestants and Jews regard these Jewish religious works as "non-canonical." That is they are important, but
slightly less-than-biblical. One of these works, that of Yeshua ben Sira,
or Sirach, was composed within two hundred years of the birth of
Jesus of Nazareth. It is composed of aphorisms or sayings, many of
which condense the riches of Hebrew tradition.

This text recalls and sharpens the vision of the all-seeing God portrayed in many of the psalms. It is a personal choice to keep the commandments, to do God's will, to choose life over death. God respects
our choices and finally confronts us with the consequences of what we
choose. We face daily the choice between life and death, usually on a
small scale, but sometimes on a large one. The wise observer will
choose loyalty to God, and life.

### Responsorial Psalm: Psalm 119:1–2, 4–5, 17–18, 33–34

### Second Reading: 1 Corinthians 2:6–10
*God has revealed this wisdom to us through the Spirit.*

Advising the complex and combative church at Corinth, Paul uses
language that can only be appreciated by those who feel that they belong. Persons who are not already sympathetic to Paul's words are
likely to judge them arrogant. He writes that the spiritually mature
have been given a secret wisdom. The so-called "wisdom" that pre-
vails in the world's institutions can only lead to destruction. What *we*
proclaim, however, is God's own wisdom, hidden before now, made
available to us for the first time in history.

Paul is addressing passionate, enthusiastic Christians who hunger
for an intellectual and ethical framework to direct their energies. He
critiques habits and ways of thinking that these new and highly in-

telligent and combative Christians must set aside. He reminds the Corinthians, and us, of our obligation to do justice and make peace.

## Gospel: Matthew 5:17–37
*I have come...to fulfill...the law and the prophets.*

The sermon on the mount begins with the beatitudes, which may give us warm, cuddly feelings. It proceeds to detail Jesus' insistence that we are salt of the earth and light of the world. Each of these images lends itself to a wide variety of interpretations, and both may confuse, even if they please us. In these verses that follow immediately, however, we collide with one of the most difficult aspects of Jesus' teaching. In this long text Jesus insists that not one letter of the law will pass away until all is fulfilled. Exploring three of the commandments, he seems to intensify the ancient injunctions against killing, adultery, and swearing falsely. His demands seem nearly impossible. Who can avoid anger, for example? Given the findings of modern psychology, what healthy person could possibly seek to avoid anger entirely?

But the sermon on the mount is not a psychological tract, nor is Jesus an analyst or counselor in the contemporary sense. Most of all, Jesus is concerned with holiness. It is a distinctly Jewish notion that Christians too often take for granted. We should not. Holiness requires prayer and fasting and other "spiritual disciplines," to be sure, but, even more important, it demands constant action on behalf of justice and peace. These are the core concerns of the law and the prophets. Here Jesus teaches that it is not enough to obey the letter of the law. We must also burn with a passion for justice and peace and righteousness, a passion through which we resemble our God and enact God's will. In order to live this passion, we must allow ourselves to be purified. We must seek only to do God's will. It is difficult indeed to live the gospel.

## Questions for Reflection

•What important choices face you now, or will face you in the near future? How can you base your decisions upon your best sense of God's will?

•How do you practice holiness? What new demands does God seem to be placing on you?

•What is the most difficult thing for you as you try to live the gospel? What sort of help do you need? How will you ask for help? Whom will you ask for help?

# Seventh Sunday in Ordinary Time

*Pray for your enemies*

*[February 18, 1996; Omitted in 1999 and 2002]*

### First Reading: Leviticus 19:1–2, 17–18

*You shall love your neighbor as yourself.*

Chapter 19 of the book of Leviticus is often called the "holiness code" because it is that portion of the law of Moses that most frequently repeats the statement, "Be holy, for I, the Lord, your God, am holy." The first pair of verses in this text sets the stage for what follows. As tradition informs us, the Lord said to Moses, "Assemble the people and tell them to be holy, and tell them how to be holy." The second pair of verses presents what most observers recognize as the core of the holiness code: Act justly and kindly, and love your neighbor as yourself.

It is clear that the notion of loving one's neighbor as oneself did not originate with Jesus (Matthew 22:39; Mark 12:31; see also Luke 10:27). Scholars debate the date of composition of the material in Leviticus, some insisting that parts of the holiness code reflect "primitive" sensibilities, while others see it as a coherent and sophisticated whole. Nearly everyone agrees, however, that the dramatic setting of the love command, at the core of the holiness code, reflects its importance in Jewish law and life.

### Responsorial Psalm: Psalm 103:1–2, 3–4, 8, 10, 12–13

### Second Reading: 1 Corinthians 3:16–23

*You are the temple of God.*

Continuing his clear statement of principles for the Corinthian church, Paul reminds them, and us, that we are temples of God. The verses that immediately precede this text compare the work of Paul and other apostles to the activities of builders. Paul has been chosen to be the master builder, to lay a foundation, and others have built upon it. The quality of any such work must be evaluated in terms of its durability, especially in its capacity to survive fire.

Paul insists that we are temples of God, that the Spirit of God dwells within us. God will destroy anyone who destroys God's temple. At this very early stage in the formation of Christian doctrine, Paul holds up to clear standards, all teaching that calls itself "Christian."

## Gospel: Matthew 5:38–48
### *Offer no resistance to injury.*

In this continuation of the sermon on the mount, Jesus intensifies things even more than he has already done. He continues to teach with the formula, "You have heard the commandment.... But my command to you is...." Earlier in the sermon (5:17–37; see the 6th Sunday in ordinary time, year A), Jesus has used familiar commandments as starting points for his challenging teaching. In this text he uses laws that are obscure, primitive, and which reflect the tribal origins of the Hebrew people.

First, Jesus replaces the law specifying "An eye for an eye, a tooth for a tooth," insisting instead that the disciple must not resist injury. He or she must turn the other cheek, making it very difficult for an assailant to continue striking. He or she must also give more than what is requested. Next, Jesus dismisses as mere paganism the law that encourages prayer for friends and hatred for enemies. Disciples must pray for their enemies. They must become perfect even as God is perfect.

We must not impose our modern notions of "perfection" upon Matthew's ancient and literary usage. This word is most likely a connection with 5:20, which insists that the disciple practice a more profound righteousness than is possible with a mere letter-of-the-law attitude. Even so, it is extremely difficult to be Christian. This text and the verses that precede it insist that we are "perfected" in holiness only when we serve, when we show mercy, when we make peace and do justice, and when we love others as we love ourselves.

## Questions for Reflection

•How often do you give more than what is asked of you or go the extra mile? How often do you respond to violent words or actions by turning the other cheek?

•What must you do to pray for your enemies? How often do you do this? What keeps you from praying for your enemies more often than you do?

•What changes would you have to make to fulfill the demands that Jesus appears to place upon all disciples? How hard will it be to make the necessary changes? What help do you need? Whose help do you need?

# EIGHTH SUNDAY IN ORDINARY TIME

## God provides

*[Omitted in 1996, 1999, and 2002]*

### First Reading: Isaiah 49:14–15

*I will never forget you.*

These two verses from the poet known as "second Isaiah" portray an unforgettable image. Think of the average mother with her baby. Can you imagine anything, or any reason, that would cause her to forget her baby? But God's love for Zion, the chosen people, is even more passionate than a mother's love. God will never forget the chosen.

This same poet often uses analogy to portray God's characteristics (see Isaiah 40:11; 51:6; 54:6; and 55:10–11) in order to help us to see God in ways that resemble but also surpass us. The poet tells us that if we want to know what God is like, we should look at the best in the human person. Whatever good we can find there, God is much more so.

### Responsorial Psalm: Psalm 62:2–3, 6–7, 8–9

### Second Reading: 1 Corinthians 4:1–5

*The Lord is the one to judge me.*

Paul tells the "brothers" at Corinth that "we" should be regarded as Christ's servants and administrators of God's mysteries. Both of these terms are meant to embrace all Christians. Of course, the sisters at Corinth and everywhere are part of the "we" who are the church. This text does not examine either servanthood or mystery, because the apostle assumes that his first audience understands both. Today, however, we might require some explanation.

The "mysteries" refer not only to Christian teachings, but also, and more importantly, to the liturgical actions that accompany teachings or the sacraments. It is easy for us today to recognize our responsibility as the community that administers the mysteries, but Paul sees servanthood as equally essential. We are, therefore, the community that serves, even as we teach and celebrate the mysteries. Paul also expresses his disdain for any judgment but the final one, and he describes his conscience as neither burdened nor innocent.

This text follows Paul's powerful critique of some of the practices of the Corinthian church (chapter 3), and its point seems to occur in verse 5: Stop passing judgment. After all, we are servants of Christ and administrators of God's mysteries. There is but one judge, a judge wiser and more just than we could ever be. This focus on God saves Paul's occasionally harsh sounding argument from the dangers of elitism. The Christian is both servant and steward, accountable to Christ and to no one else.

### Gospel: Matthew 6:24–34
*Your heavenly Father knows all that you need.*

Jesus poses two figures in the middle of the sermon on the mount, and they make a single point. In the first, he harpoons money and its advantages as so many idols. We must not allow any of these to become our master. This figure reminds us of the single-heartedness that Jesus has encouraged in the beatitudes (5:8), but it also echoes 1 Corinthians 4:1–5. With a second figure Jesus introduces an analogy, much in the manner of "second Isaiah." God feeds the birds and clothes them and garbs the fields in a splendor that exceeds even the fabled Solomon in all his glory. God provides for you far more than for your surroundings (see Genesis 1:26–31). Worry accomplishes nothing. Worse yet, it is an example of bad faith. Earlier in the sermon Jesus has invited everyone into discipleship and insisted upon the most pure of motives behind the disciple's every thought and action. Here he assures us with a thought that remains consistent with everything taught earlier: Trust your whole life to God, because God provides.

### Questions for Reflection

•How is your relationship with your mother? What is, or what was, the relationship like? How is your relationship with your father? What are the best things your parents have given to you or done for you? What do these best things suggest about God's love for you?

•Why does Paul speak of servanthood and our care of God's mysteries in a single phrase? How well do Catholics in general tend to balance their servanthood and their care of the mysteries? How well do you accomplish this balance? What must you change? How can or should the church change?

•What worries you? How important a place does worry hold in your thinking and action? On the other hand, how does God provide for you? What does God provide? What changes must you make? How will you make these changes? What support will help you to make them?

# NINTH SUNDAY IN ORDINARY TIME

*Words into practice*

*[Omitted in 1996, 1999, and 2002]*

### First Reading: Deuteronomy 11:18, 26–28

*Take these words...into your heart and soul.*

The book of Deuteronomy consists of three speeches or homilies, a recitation of God's laws and description of blessings and rituals, and a description of the end of Moses' life. All these things occur at the end of Israel's wanderings. Far more than a recitation of history, the book creates a great drama. At the brink of the promised land Moses teaches the people. Deuteronomy is thus a summary and a climax of Moses' career, and of the "law of Moses." This book was almost certainly written during or immediately after the Jews' exile in Babylon. Knowing this, we can see that Deuteronomy interprets the seven centuries of history that elapsed between Moses' death and the book's composition.

These verses occur toward the end of the second homily, just before Moses recites various divine commands. Here he gives an instruction and a choice. If the people obey the law, they will be blessed. If they disobey the law, they therefore choose foreign gods. This choice will bring a curse upon their heads.

### Responsorial Psalm: Psalm 31:2–3, 3–4, 17, 25

### Second Reading: Romans 3:21–25a, 28

*A person is justified by faith.*

For Paul, the law and the prophets bear witness to God's justice, which is accomplished in Jesus Christ and made available to all who believe. The bedrock doctrine of Christianity is underlined in verses 25–26: We are all undeservedly justified, cleansed through the blood of Jesus Christ. Paul concludes this argument by insisting that Christ justifies us, apart from the law.

Throughout his letters, Paul's use of the term "law" is almost always negative. Often he condemns an attitude toward the law that has little or nothing to do with Moses' exalted view of the importance of the law. Here, writing to an audience of Gentile Christians and Jewish Christians, Paul views "law" as a form of condemnation, something from which people must be freed. In so doing, he implies that a form of legalism has too often replaced the law that gives life and that guides people into holiness.

Surely Paul does not disagree with Moses, or with the Deuteronomist, or with any other great Jewish teacher. For them, the law is a life-giving thing, a guide to authentic and holy life. A person who obeys the law must do so in faith, if the law is to accomplish anything good. Paul knows this, and Moses knew this, too. We can be misled by Paul's wording, however, if we are careless. In any case, Jesus has given all a gift that no one can earn. We are justified by faith.

### Gospel: Matthew 7:21–27

*...one who does the will of my Father in heaven*
*...will enter the kingdom of God....*

Concluding the sermon on the mount, Jesus distinguishes between mere religious observance and genuine faith. Not everyone who cries "Lord, Lord," or who says any of the other proper words, will enter the kingdom of God. If all we do is follow the rules and forms of religion, we go nowhere. Real faith puts Jesus' words into practice.

Jesus paints two images to bring the difference into focus. Putting his words into practice is like building a house on a solid foundation. Such a house can withstand any storm. But failure to enact Jesus' words is like building a house on sand. The first storm collapses the house.

At the conclusion and climax of Matthew's masterful summary of Jesus' teaching, Jesus seems to echo the great ancient teacher, Moses. Take these words into your heart and soul. Make them your own, and live by them. You are blessed. You are light for the world. Don't just obey the commandments, but live them completely. Think, talk, and act with the purest of motives. Don't worry, for God provides. And always do the will of the Father.

### Questions for Reflection

•Where do you find God's law? Where does church teaching tell us to look for God's law? How do you respond to this law?

•Who or what sets us free? Why can't Christians just take this truth and ignore any consideration of law?

•How well do you balance the words of your faith with action? How do you think you can improve? What would someone who knows and loves you tell you that you must do to strike a faithful balance between words and action? If you do not have an honest answer to this question, take the steps necessary to find one.

# Tenth Sunday in Ordinary Time

*Follow me*

*[Omitted in 1996, 1999, and 2002]*

### First Reading: Hosea 6:3–6

*...it is love that I desire, not sacrifice.*

These verses are notable not only for their message, but also for their structure, which is itself a part of the message. They represent Hebrew poetry, which rhymes, but not in the manner of English verse. Hebrew poetry usually consists of doublets that rhyme logically. Words in a second line might not sound at all like the words of a first line. The second line does, however, repeat and deepen the thought expressed in the first. Sometimes, as in the case of this text's verse 3, there are three lines, all expressing a single thought. In Hebrew as in English, a three-line structure stands out. It asks for, and receives, more attention than the doublets that surround it. This text is a simple and perfect introduction to Hebrew poetry.

It is also classic prophecy. Hosea's argument is straightforward: God is coming, as surely as the dawn, and this means judgment. God comes like the rain, permeating the earth. What can be done with you? Your piety evaporates, like the morning dew. This is why the prophets have spoken God's punishing words. God demands love and intimacy with God, not empty pieties.

### Responsorial Psalm: Psalm 50:1, 8, 12–13, 14–15

### Second Reading: Romans 4:18–25

*...his faith was credited to him as justice.*

Paul evokes the memory of Abraham. Abraham is the great exemplar of faith, never questioning or doubting God's promise. This is the kind of faith God requires of Christians, a faith in Jesus, who was executed for our sins and who has been raised for our justification.

The centerpiece of the text is Paul's use of Genesis 15:5: "his faith was credited to him as righteousness [or justice]." Abraham is important as an ancestor with countless descendants, but he is far more important as an example. Paul appreciates the heroism in Abram's response to the first stirrings that would lead him to leave home to seek an unknown God in the wilderness. He understands that the divine promise of descendants must have seemed absurd to the aged Abraham, yet he never doubted. Paul commends this kind of faith to the Christians in Rome, and to us.

### Gospel: Matthew 9:9–13
*Follow me.*

As portrayed in Matthew 7:21–27, Jesus concludes the sermon on the mount with a challenge: Put my words into practice. And as we might expect, he is better than anyone at putting his own words into practice. In Matthew's chapter 8 and in the beginning of chapter 9, Jesus keeps very busy doing just that. He works cures, calms a storm, and expels demons. In all these acts he shows us what it is to live a perfect balance between faithful words and faithful actions. For Jesus, as for the biblical heroes who have inspired him, faith always becomes word and action.

We might wish to excuse ourselves from any effort to copy Jesus' heroics. After all, most of us cannot effect miraculous cures. Nor can we calm storms, and we hardly ever think of demons, let alone try to expel them. But in this text, Jesus does something that any human person is able to do. Even though he uses no extra-human power, his action is still extraordinary. He sees a man named Matthew collecting taxes. In Jesus' time, nearly everyone hated tax collectors, Jews who had sold out their own people to work for Caesar and gained untold riches by charging far more than required. Jesus says, "Follow me," and Matthew obeys. Like Jesus, Matthew acts immediately and credibly upon Jesus' word, but this causes a problem. Observers complain about the company Jesus keeps, and his response strips away all formalities: "I am here for the sick and the sinners." He urges his critics to ponder the words cited in today's first reading: "I desire mercy, not piety." Jesus thus speaks and acts as prophet, holy man, and faithful Jew.

### Questions for Reflection

•What is piety? When is piety empty? When is it real and believable? What sort of piety do you practice? What does God expect of you? What does God demand from all Christians, and from the church?

•How is your faith? What result or action illustrates your faith?

•What do you think about the company Jesus keeps? Who are the Matthews and other tax-collectors of today? Whom does Jesus call to follow him?

•How do you respond to Jesus' call? What, if anything, is keeping you from dropping everything to follow him?

# ELEVENTH SUNDAY IN ORDINARY TIME

*Announce the kingdom*

[June 16, 1996; June 13, 1999; June 16, 2002]

### First Reading: Exodus 19:2–6a

*...you shall be to me a kingdom of priests, a holy nation.*

During forty years in the wilderness God appears to Israel three times at Mt. Sinai. This text sets the stage for the first appearance. God speaks to Moses from behind the clouds shrouding the mountain, and the words interpret the events that the people remember: "You were delivered from the Egyptians, and carried safely through the desert, as if on eagle's wings. I brought you to me. Listen to my voice and keep my covenant. You will be my pride and my joy, my favorite people whom I love above all the peoples of the earth. Live my word and keep the covenant. You will be a kingdom of priests, a holy people."

These verses do not date from the exodus itself, but from some seven hundred years later, during the exile in Babylon. They represent the chosen people's efforts to understand why they, of all people, have had to suffer. The answer, developed during the exile and in the years immediately following the Jews' return to the promised land, lies in the people's repeated failures to keep the covenant and to live God's word. Israel is responsible to God to be the example for all the nations of the world. Biblical authors and editors have underlined this responsibility by placing it in a story of God's self-revelation at Sinai.

### Responsorial Psalm: Psalm 100:1–2, 3, 5

### Second Reading: Romans 5:6–11

*Christ died for us.*

Paul identifies Christ's two-fold accomplishment. His death has justified us; his resurrection has saved us. Paul's logic creates analogies similar to those of "second Isaiah" (Isaiah 40–55; see for example 40:11; 51:6; 54:6; 55:10–11). We might imagine someone dying for the sake of a good person, but Christ died for the sake of even the most wretched of us. Paul's thinking continues: "If you can imagine that Christ has died for you, it is far more certain that he offers you salvation. Moreover, you may rejoice, even boast. "

---

## Gospel: Matthew 9:36–10:8

*...he...gave them authority to expel unclean spirits
and cure sickness and disease.*

Since the end of the sermon on the mount Jesus has been very busy curing people and keeping company with notorious and probably very lonely sinners. Now he surveys the crowd and sees overwhelming need. Since ancient times the church has regarded this episode as a turning point in Jesus' work. Staring at the enormity of human need, Jesus comes face-to-face with his own human limits. He can and does accomplish salvation on behalf of all, but no one human person, not even Jesus, can bandage every wound, soothe every hurt, or stem the advances of every disease. For this task, Jesus needs deputies, people who will act in his place, and in every place.

Matthew describes this commissioning in a way that parallels similar descriptions in the gospel accounts of Mark (6:10ff) and Luke (9:1–6). This account also includes material unique to Matthew: Jesus instructs the disciples to avoid pagan territory and to concentrate their energies on the lost sheep of Israel. This instruction is consistent with Matthew's concern for the Jews, and with the probability that this account was written for first-century Jews who have accepted the Christian way.

Jesus' final instruction might be called a "word-deed": "Announce the kingdom and free the hearers from all infirmities." The act of announcing the kingdom must be done in word and in deed. Since the beginning, healing has been the basic movement in announcing the kingdom. It is the core of who we are—the church. It is our job.

## Questions for Reflection

•What are the signs of human need? What sorts of things need healing, curing, mending, feeding, clothing, cleansing, or liberating? What needs can you identify in your household, neighborhood, town, region, nation, and world? When you consider human need, how do you feel?

•How do you usually respond when you consider the enormity of human need? How does Jesus respond? How does his response contrast with yours? How is it similar? How does Jesus' response to human need place a claim upon you?

•You have received a gift. How do you use this gift to give to others? How do you announce the kingdom? How do you heal? How can you do a better job announcing the kingdom and healing?

# TWELFTH SUNDAY IN ORDINARY TIME
### God is always with us
*[June 23, 1996; June 20, 1999; June 23, 2002]*

### First Reading: Jeremiah 20:10–13
*But the Lord is with me.*

In one of many reflective moments, the prophet Jeremiah utters what is actually a psalm concerning his life and work. In this text we enter the psalm following verses describing the difficult nature of Jeremiah's message, his suffering on behalf of the message, his reluctance to continue, and the irresistible force that keeps him going. When he tries to keep God's word bottled up inside him, it becomes like a fire in his bones. He cannot endure it.

Aware of whispers all around him, Jeremiah knows that former friends want to trap him and take revenge. But he knows that the Lord is with him, fighting like a mighty champion. Whatever may befall the prophet, the Lord has rescued the poor from the wicked, and will do so again and again.

### Responsorial Psalm: Psalm 69:8–10, 14, 17, 33–35

### Second Reading: Romans 5:12–15
*But the gift is not like the offense.*

Centuries ago, Martin Luther used Romans 5:15 as a basis for his critique of corruption in the church. He made many important and valuable points, some of which Rome was at first not prepared to hear. Many of Luther's critiques led directly to the work of the council of Trent, which gave shape to the Roman Catholicism we know today. No reasonable Catholic would disagree with the truth that we are saved by grace alone. It is one of history's cruel ironies that the Christian world had to fracture into many pieces over this point.

Since Paul first wrote this text, it has always issued a firm reminder to all its readers. It is God's grace alone that saves us. In something like a symmetry, Christ has undone the mistake of Adam. Through Adam, death entered the world, and now Christ has made available to all the possibility of eternal life. Christ has reversed Adam's fault.

But Christ's gift is not exactly like the offense. We do not measure the things of grace. Adam's sin caused countless generations to live in the thrall of death and sin. Even today, billions remain enslaved. Christ's gift, offered freely to everyone, gives life, forever.

## Gospel: Matthew 10:26–33

*Do not be afraid of anything.*

In chapter 10 of Matthew's account of the gospel, Jesus speaks about the mission of the twelve apostles. He has given them authority to cast out spirits and afflictions (see Matthew 9:36–10:8, the gospel for the eleventh Sunday in ordinary time). He also speaks in detail about the mission of the twelve apostles. They must travel among "the lost sheep of the house of Israel," announcing the kingdom of heaven, healing the sick, raising the dead, cleansing lepers, and driving out demons. They must do all of this without any payment, staying only where they are welcomed. In short, they must follow Jesus' example.

This text places us in the middle of this long episode. Jesus teaches the Twelve, and us, with regard to our work. Don't let anyone intimidate you. Do not fear someone who can take life from your body but who cannot touch the soul. The apostle must proclaim out loud in daylight what was whispered in the dark. To disown Jesus is to be disowned before the Father. Like Jeremiah, the apostle must speak, no matter what. The apostle has no choice but to announce the kingdom and to heal.

In the middle of all these challenges, Jesus also speaks consoling words. God loves us and watches over us. Every hair of our heads has been counted. We should not be afraid, nor in any event allow our fears to deter us from what we must do. God is always with us.

## Questions for Reflection

•What sorts of things drive you? What things do you do because you feel that you must do them? What are the "musts" that claim your time and energy and that seem to leave you no other choice?

•When you examine the "musts" that drive you, how large a role do you find God playing in your life? Ask the same question in another way: How many of the things that drive you really are "musts"? What changes can you make?

•What fears limit your efforts to announce the kingdom and to heal? What does Jesus say to your fears? What does Jesus demand of you, in spite of your fears?

# THIRTEENTH SUNDAY
# IN ORDINARY TIME

## Welcoming Christ, dying with Christ

*[June 30, 1996; June 27, 1999; June 30, 2002]*

### First Reading: 2 Kings 4:8–11, 14–16

*I know that he is a holy man of God.*

This text evokes the cycle of stories concerning Elisha the prophet and a Shunammite woman "of influence." First she invites him to dine with her, and the invitation becomes a custom they will observe each time Elisha passes through. Later she persuades her aging husband to build a room for Elisha atop the house. To express his gratitude, Elisha promises that she will have a son.

Later in the story-cycle the woman scoffs at this preposterous notion and yet she bears a son. Some years later, the son complains of a headache and dies. The woman rushes to Elisha, who sends his assistant Gehazi with Elisha's staff. Gehazi is unable to do anything, however, and Elisha himself goes and revives the boy (4:18–37).

### Responsorial Psalm: Psalm 89:2–3, 16–17, 18–19

### Second Reading: Romans 6:3–4, 8–11

*We were buried with him.*

These verses are proclaimed every year at the Easter Vigil. Their explanation of the significance of baptism provides a foundation for all of our sacramental theology. For Paul, baptism is far more than a cleansing or a renewal, more even than a public celebration of one's decision to allow his or her life to be reformed. When we are baptized we are really buried with Jesus Christ. We are also raised with him, given a new life in which sin holds no power over us.

In early Christian centuries, people were baptized only after the most careful consideration. Just before dawn they were baptized. When they emerged from the water they were anointed, dried off, and clothed in white. Now for the first time they would join the assembly to break bread. When Paul spoke of dying and entering a new life with Christ, these people felt the power in his words.

With the modern catechumenate the church has moved to place the robust and risky movements of baptism back where they belong, at the center of our lives. The church invites us to experience baptism as a powerful, life-changing passage, and not as a weak, ineffectual ritual. It invites us to immerse ourselves in Christ.

## Gospel: Matthew 10:37–42
*If you do not take up your cross, you are not worthy of me....*
Here we find Jesus at his most strident, giving us a very difficult message: "If you love your family more than me, or if you do not take up your cross and come after me you are not worthy of me." He teaches that when we seek ourselves, we waste our time, but when we give up everything for him, we discover who we are.

This paradox stands at the core of our faith. The way to life leads through the scandalous and painful death embodied by the cross. There is no avoiding this most difficult message. But among these demanding statements, Jesus appears open to what we might today call "ecumenism." If we welcome the disciple, a holy person, or a missionary (one of the "lowly ones"), we receive a divine reward. Like the woman at Shunem receiving Elisha, prophet of a foreign faith, we do God's work by assisting God's assistants.

## Questions for Reflection
•Why do many Christians today take baptism for granted? Why is baptism almost never at the center of our lives? What church practices seem to work against baptism as a pivotal, life-changing event? What church practices seem to want to restore baptism to its rightful place?

•How can you reclaim your baptism? What promises did you make at baptism, or what promises were made on your behalf? How well do you live up to these promises? What can you change?

•How important is it that you take up your cross to follow Jesus? How will you do it?

# FOURTEENTH SUNDAY IN ORDINARY TIME

### The king's burden

*[July 7, 1996; July 4, 1999; July 7, 2002]*

### First Reading: Zechariah 9:9–10

*Your king shall come to you.*

The prophet urges the Jewish people to rejoice because the king is coming. In an image that contrasts greatly with the actions of the warrior-God depicted immediately before these verses, the king is meek. He will ride a young donkey, a modest beast that is hardly a warrior's steed. Although he is meek, the king is not without power. He will banish all the machines of war and will proclaim peace to the nations. He shall reign over a territory that reaches to the ends of the earth. Such a king must have enormous power and authority. The paradox is that this most powerful king comes in meekness and humility.

### Responsorial Psalm: Psalm 145:1–2, 8–9, 10–11, 13–14

### Second Reading: Romans 8:9, 11–13

*If you do not have the Spirit of Christ, you do not belong to Christ.*

Paul's language, which sets flesh and spirit in opposition, can sometimes cause problems for us because we tend to limit our reading of the word "flesh" to sexual matters. For Paul, however, everything can and should be understood in terms of Christ's passage through death into glorified life. The flesh is what human life would be without God. The Spirit of God is the source of life. Alone, the flesh is corrupt, worthless, dead. Living "according to the flesh" is no life at all. It is sin, corruption, death. It is the pretense that we can live on our own terms, without God, that we can give ourselves life. Life "in the Spirit," on the other hand, recognizes our utter dependence upon God. It is incorruptible and eternal.

### Gospel: Matthew 11:25–30

*Come to me, all you who are weary.*

Here are two disjointed sayings, possibly intended to echo portions of the books of Sirach and Proverbs. The first seems to be a prayer. Jesus praises the Father for revealing to persons with little or no schooling truths concealed from the learned. Matthew has reworked older material, perhaps to illustrate the deep gulf between Jews who followed Christ and other Jews who did not. The point is sharpened with the words "no one knows the Father but the Son—and anyone to whom the Son wishes to reveal him."

The second saying echoes an invitation extended by Wisdom, a manifestation of God described in the newer Hebrew books in our Bible (see Wisdom 6:12–16, 32nd Sunday in ordinary time, year A; Wisdom 7:7–11, 28th Sunday in ordinary time, year B; Proverbs 9:1–6, 20th Sunday in ordinary time, year B; Wisdom 9:13–18, 23rd Sunday in ordinary time, year C). Clearly some early Christian thinkers, including Matthew, have identified Jesus with personified Wisdom. "Come...I will refresh you...my yoke is easy, my burden is light."

Jesus the king differs from all other kings. Where most kings demand tribute and other forms of taxes, Jesus imposes a lighter burden. Where other kings live in splendor among riches, Jesus associates with sinners and the sick and the lame. Where other kings ride war horses as they lead their armies into battle, Jesus rides a donkey and asks that we take up our cross to follow him. But, as the first reading tells us, this is the real king, the only one who brings peace to the nations.

### Questions for Reflection
•What images come to mind when you hear the word "king"? How does the first reading compare or contrast with your images?

•When you live according to the flesh (we all do, sometimes), what sorts of things do you do? What specific things do you do when you live "in the Spirit?"

•What does Jesus the king demand of you? How do you feel his yoke? What impact does his burden impose upon you?

# FIFTEENTH SUNDAY IN ORDINARY TIME

*Water and seed and soil*

*[July 14, 1996; July 11, 1999; July 14, 2002]*

### First Reading: Isaiah 55:10–11

*My word shall not return to me empty.*

Here is a brilliant image from one of the greatest of all poets, the anonymous prophet known as "second Isaiah." Water describes the movements and effects of God's word. In various forms water descends from the sky. As snow and ice, water delights the eye and shapes mountains. Flowing ever downhill, water forms rivulets, brooks, and eventually mighty streams that reach the ocean. Some water stays in lakes and wetlands, and some seeps into the ground. It waters the earth and gives life. Water achieves its purpose when it gives seed to the one who sows, and bread to everyone who eats. God's word follows a similar pattern by achieving God's purposes for us.

### Responsorial Psalm: Psalm 65:10, 11, 12–13, 14

### Second Reading: Romans 8:18–23

*We have the Spirit as first fruits.*

Having distinguished between "the flesh" and the Spirit that animates what is otherwise inert (Romans 8:9, 11–13, 14th Sunday in ordinary time, year A), Paul reflects upon the suffering he endured in Rome. Because we live in the Spirit, he says, present sufferings are nothing compared to the glory that awaits. Creation has been subjected to sin and death, but ultimately the Spirit will free the whole world from corruption. The pains we can see so readily in the world are labor pains. The first fruits of these pains is the Spirit, whose work has only begun.

These ancient words seem as fresh today as they were when Paul first wrote them. We are invited to breathe the Spirit and to work on freeing the world.

## Gospel: Matthew 13:1–23

*A farmer went out to sow some seed.*

The press of the crowd having forced him to preach toward shore while standing in a boat, Jesus speaks in parables. One is presented here. A farmer went out to sow seed. Some seed fell on the road, and birds came to eat this up. Some seed fell on rocky ground, where it sprouted quickly but soon withered in the sun for lack of roots. Still other seed fell among thorns, which grew up and choked it. Part of the seed fell upon good soil, where it produced grain up to a hundred-fold.

In this crowded scene, the disciples manage to ask Jesus privately why he teaches in parables. He tells them that they are privileged to know mysteries not made available to others. Citing the prophet's indictment of a people who do not use their senses to hear or to see (Isaiah 52:15), he assures the disciples that they see and hear what has been kept hidden from prophets and saints. Then Jesus explains the parable of the sower. The various soils represent differing ways in which we might receive the seed that is God's word.

The Word is always the same. It always bears within itself the promise of abundant life. Some people have so hardened themselves that the Word merely bounces off their surfaces. Others respond with immediate enthusiasm that wears thin before long. Still others surround themselves with so much clutter that the Word cannot grow to maturity in them. Finally, some people do what they must to receive the Word, having allowed themselves to be tilled, weeded, and watered. The receptive person understands the Word, allows it to grow roots, and organizes his or her priorities so that the Word is far more important than anything else.

## Questions for Reflection

•What are the many good things that water accomplishes in our world? In what ways does water destroy? Why is water an especially good representation of God's word?

•Why is suffering valuable? How can suffering be an important part of human life? How have you suffered? How does the world suffer? What keeps you going, even though suffering exists?

•What sort of soil do you provide for the seed that is God's word? What do the fruits you yield tell you and the world? What sort of soil would you prefer to be? What must you do to prepare the soil?

# SIXTEENTH SUNDAY IN ORDINARY TIME

*The reign of God is like....*

[July 21, 1996; July 18, 1999; July 21, 2002]

### First Reading: Wisdom 12:13, 16–19

*There is no god besides you.*

Written only a few years before Jesus' lifetime, the book of Wisdom appears to be a summary and encouragement for Jews living in Alexandria. Surrounded by the intellectual and religious currents of a major foreign city, many Jews of the time required a clear, concise guide supporting faithful practice of their religion. The book of Wisdom seems to have served as the "catechism" they required.

Today's text both addresses God and instructs the reader about God. There is only one God who has care of all, and who is always fair, just, and impartial. God holds power over everything and is lenient to all. Through God's enduring lenience the people can hope that their sins will be forgiven.

### Responsorial Psalm: Psalm 86:5–6, 9–10, 15–16

### Second Reading: Romans 8:26–27

*We do not know how to pray as we ought.*

We do not know how to pray, any more than Roman Christians did in the first century. But the Spirit assists us, making intercession on our behalf with "groanings which cannot be expressed in speech." Even though we are inarticulate, God understands all prayer that is guided by the Spirit.

Some persons use this text to insist upon the practice of *glossolalia*, or "speaking in tongues." Paul's view seems less narrowly-focused. Because the Spirit may prompt us in a variety of expressions, groanings are only one type of inspired prayer. Everything depends on God. God, who searches hearts, hears all kinds of prayer, overcoming any of our inadequacies.

### Gospel: Matthew 13:24–43

*Let everyone heed these words.*

Immediately following the parable of the sower (Matthew 13:1–23), Jesus offers three more parables and an explanation. The reign of God is like a person who sowed good seed. An enemy planted weeds among the seed at night, and the servants wondered whether the weeds should be pulled out. The owner replied that everything should be left to grow, so that at the harvest the wheat will be gathered to the barn while the weeds will be burned.

The reign of God is also like a mustard seed, the smallest of all seeds, which grows into the largest of shrubs. And the reign of God is like yeast kneaded into flour, causing the whole to rise.

We might wish to quarrel with some details. A gardener who does not weed, for instance, virtually guarantees that the desired plants will never grow to their full size or fruitfulness. It is also not clear which "mustard seed" is intended, among the many thousands of mustards that populate our earth. On the other hand, Jesus is not delivering a treatise on agriculture. The type of seed matters far less than its growth from tiny to enormous. And maybe the weeds are left because, after all, that's life. We do not grow in isolation, and certainly not in conditions that we always find favorable. Our lives are full of weeds, and maybe we ought to get used to that.

Because Jesus teaches in parables from this point on, the disciples ask for an explanation. He interprets the roles of farmer, field, seed, weeds, and enemy, predicting the end of the world. Those who are weeds will be uprooted from the kingdom and destroyed, while saints will shine like the sun in the Father's kingdom.

## Questions for Reflection

•How easy is it for you to agree that God is always fair, just, and impartial? Why would you take issue with this statement? In your family, in your town, in your nation, in the world, what evidence might lead you to question God's fairness, justice, or impartiality? What is a creative way in which you can use the questions you raise?

•How do you pray? How do you think you ought to pray? When does your prayer seem most genuine?

•What is the reign of God like? In addition to a sower, a mustard seed, and yeast, what other images could you use to describe God's reign? Why do these images work? What truths do they tell?

# SEVENTEENTH SUNDAY IN ORDINARY TIME

## *The reign of God*

[July 28, 1996; July 25, 1999; July 28, 2002]

### First Reading: 1 Kings 3:5, 7–12

*Ask for something...and I will give it to you.*

Before building the temple of the Lord and the wall around Jerusalem, Solomon had offered sacrifices on the high places. Coming to him in a dream at Gibeon, now God asks the young king what he desires. Overwhelmed by the challenges of governance, Solomon asks for an understanding heart to judge God's people and distinguish right from wrong. Pleased that Solomon has not requested riches or a long life, God promises him a heart so wise and understanding that no one before or since would be his equal.

Looking back through the centuries, we might well ask how wise Solomon proved to be. After all, he was the last king to preside over twelve unified tribes. After his death, the ten northern tribes separated from the two southern tribes, creating the rival kingdoms of Israel and Judah, respectively. But what matters here is God's great gift, not Solomon's eventual use of it.

### Responsorial Psalm: Psalm 119:57, 72, 76–77, 127–128, 129–130

### Second Reading: Romans 8:28–30

*God makes all things work together for the good of those who love God.*

Paul gives us very difficult language here. Those whom God foreknew, God also predestined to share the image of the Son. Those who were predestined were also called, justified, and glorified. The notion of "predestination" has caused great confusion for Christians through history. Complicating matters, three different ancient manuscripts suggest three completely different bases upon which our modern translations can be constructed. No wonder this word confuses!

Catholics have usually preferred wording that portrays all things working together for the good of those who love God. Other wordings tend to emphasize God's foreknowledge so strongly that our choices do not seem to matter. And in nearly every other point he makes in his epistles, Paul recognizes the importance of human freedom. Here, we recognize that we can choose to love God. In so doing, we cooperate with the hopes that God holds for us.

### Gospel: Matthew 13:44–52
*The reign of God is like a buried treasure.*

Immediately following the parables of the good seed among the weeds, the mustard seed, and the yeast, Jesus illustrates the reign of God with three other comparisons. God's reign is like a buried treasure in a field. Upon finding it, a man sells everything to buy the field. The reign of God is also like a merchant's search for fine pearls. Finding a truly valuable specimen, he sells everything he owns in order to buy it.

But God's reign is also like a dragnet. Hauled through the lake and onto the shore, the net contains valuable things to be salvaged as well as much that is worthless. At the end of the world, the wicked and the just will be separated. In the meantime, we all live together, dragged through the waters in the same net.

Jesus concludes this collection of parables with another comparison. The scribe who is learned in the reign of God is like the head of the household who can bring forth both old and new from storage. While we live in a world full of weeds and rotted fish, we must learn to choose what is truly valuable. We must think and act always in terms of the reign of God, a kingdom that is here, now.

### Questions for Reflection

•Why does the first reading locate wisdom and understanding in the "heart," while we tend to see these things as functions of the head? What difference does it make whether wisdom is a matter of head or of heart?

•Why does Catholic teaching insist upon human freedom? Why are our choices important? How can we exercise our freedom wisely?

•What do you have to do to become learned in the reign of God? How does this learning differ from other forms of learning? Why is it important?

# EIGHTEENTH SUNDAY IN ORDINARY TIME

## The Lord's banquet

*[August 4, 1996; August 1, 1999; August 4, 2002]*

### First Reading: Isaiah 55:1–3

*Come to the water!*

The poems that constitute chapters 40 through 55 of Isaiah are the work of an anonymous author. This cycle of poems, often called "second Isaiah," merits a place among the masterpieces of world literature.

This text presents the opening verses of the final poem. Evoking an image of a feast at an oasis in the desert, it offers an invitation: "Everyone who is thirsty, come to the water! If you have no money, come, sit, and eat. Enjoy the richest and most satisfying food and drink, at no cost. Don't waste your money on things that do not satisfy. Listen, so that you may have life through the everlasting covenant between God and the chosen people." We can find real satisfaction at the Lord's table, listening attentively to God's word.

### Responsorial Psalm: Psalm 145:8–9, 15–16, 17–18

### Second Reading: Romans 8:35, 37–39

*Who will separate us from the love of Christ?*

At the end of his extended discourse on the Spirit, Paul offers a powerful guarantee. There is nothing that separates us from the love of Christ, not trial, pain, persecution, hunger, nakedness, war, nor even death. For that matter, none of the forces invisible to us in this life can keep us from Christ's love. We ought not to make excuses.

### Gospel: Matthew 14:13–21

*All those present ate their fill....*

The chilly reception at Nazareth and the death of John the Baptizer provide a turning point for Matthew's account of the gospel. From now on, the tone of the narrative is more somber, more clearly focused on the cross. It is as if Jesus has now discovered the full cost of being the Son of God.

Today's text follows immediately after the news of John's death. Seeking time alone, Jesus is pursued by crowds. He cures their sick until nightfall, when the disciples urge him to send everyone home for dinner. Jesus insists, however, that the disciples can feed the crowd themselves. Confronted with only five loaves and two fish, the disciples protest the impossibility of the task. Jesus prays, blesses the bread and the fish, and gives them to the disciples, who distribute them to the people. And, after five thousand families have eaten their fill, twelve baskets of fragments remain.

Like the first reading, this text describes God's banquet. The settings could hardly differ more. The poetry of second Isaiah suggests an intimate setting, while the story in Matthew involves a giant crowd. The poet invites the listener to a banquet of grains, wine and milk, and rich fare. (Some translations say "delight yourselves in fatness!") Matthew describes the simpler fare of bread and fish. Even so, the two texts bear important similarities. Both describe complete satisfaction of hunger, a satisfaction that only God can provide. Each presents the banquet as a gift of food provided in abundance and without cost. The description of each banquet is surrounded by descriptions of healing that God accomplishes in the world.

Like parallel versions of the story in the other accounts of the gospel, Matthew's version of the miraculous feeding teaches about the Eucharist. It is linked with the cross, both through the extreme demands placed upon Jesus at the beginning of this text, and in the larger fabric of Matthew's account. Jesus fills us to satisfaction beyond our wildest dreams, in the feast we call Eucharist.

## Questions for Reflection

•What sorts of things do not satisfy? How often do you spend your money on them? How important do such things seem to be in our culture? By contrast, what does satisfy? What must you do to come to the table?

•What seems to separate you from the love of Christ, from time to time? Who erects these barriers? Who is responsible for them? What can you do about them?

• Why does Jesus insist that the disciples feed the crowd? What does Jesus expect us to do? What are our eucharistic responsibilities?

# NINETEENTH SUNDAY IN ORDINARY TIME

## Turning points

*[August 11, 1996; August 8, 1999; August 11, 2002]*

### First Reading: 1 Kings 19:9, 11–13

*There was a tiny whispering sound.*

Elijah has presided over a public contest between the queen's pagan god and the God of Israel, and of course the real God has won (1 Kings 18:16–40). Humiliated, the queen places a price on Elijah's head. Fleeing, Elijah hides in a cave. The verses that precede this text pose the word of God coming to Elijah and the prophet's answer: "Why are you hiding?" "I hide because I have worked very hard on God's behalf, and yet the people flirt with other gods and now my life is in danger."

Then, at God's command, the prophet stands outside the cave, where he witnesses a ferocious wind, an earthquake, and a fire. But the Lord is in none of these things. Then Elijah hears a tiny whispering sound (sometimes translated as a still, small voice). Acknowledging the presence of God, the prophet cloaks his face and stands at the mouth of the cave.

The verses following this text repeat exactly the word of the Lord coming to Elijah, and Elijah's response (see 19:9–10 and 19:13–14). But now Elijah realizes that he must come out from hiding and resume his work.

This text describes Elijah standing outside the cave, but also much more. It portrays a contest within the prophet, a contest between false and real manifestations of God. As before, the real God wins, but in an unexpected way. Sometimes we expect God to appear in spectacle, and once in a while God matches or exceeds our expectations. More often, however, God approaches us subtly. Like Elijah, we must listen among the noise and clatter in our lives for a tiny whispering sound.

### Responsorial Psalm: Psalm 85:9, 10, 11–12, 13–14

### Second Reading: Romans 9:1–5

*There is…grief and…pain in my heart.*

Paul speaks of his passion for his own Jewish people, even wishing to be separated from Christ for their sake. The Jews have been blessed uniquely among all people, but Paul is convinced that they have failed to see what has been made plain to others.

Today the church denounces any teaching of contempt for the Jews. We are not permitted under any circumstances to harm someone else as we proclaim the gospel of Christ. We must follow Paul's example and pray for and with our Jewish brothers and sisters.

## Gospel: Matthew 14:22–33
*Beyond a doubt you are the Son of God!*

After feeding the crowds, Jesus at last gets the solitude he has sought since learning of the Baptizer's death. He prays well into the night, while the disciples head across the lake in a boat. In the middle of the night Jesus rejoins them, walking across the waves.

This unusual scene sets up a dialogue in which the disciples discover who Jesus really is. At first terrified, they cry out. Jesus tells them not to fear, and he identifies himself. Wanting proof, Peter asks Jesus to tell him to walk on the water. Jesus' response is, "Come!" Walking for a few steps, Peter grows frightened, begins to sink, and cries, "Lord save me!" Extending a hand, Jesus reprimands Peter for his small faith. Finally, everyone present declares, "Beyond a doubt you are the Son of God!"

This dialogue has echoed throughout history, repeated countless times in countless lives. Our journey into faith often follows exactly this pattern. We fear, we are assured. We step out into an unfamiliar and threatening place, and we falter. And when there is nothing else left, we cry out, Christ rescues us, and we then believe.

## Questions for Reflection

•How often has God touched you in spectacular or dramatic events? How often has God approached you more subtly? How do you listen?

•How do you determine whether God really is calling upon you? When God asks you to take a risk, how do you respond?

•Where and how did your faith begin? What steps have you taken since this beginning? What steps have you not yet taken? How often have you been afraid? How often have you called out to Jesus, in utter dependence? Where are you, in your journey into faith?

# TWENTIETH SUNDAY IN ORDINARY TIME

*Great faith*

[August 18, 1996; Omitted 1999; August 18, 2002]

### First Reading: Isaiah 56:1, 6, 7

*Observe what is right, do what is just.*

Evidence suggests that the poet who created chapters 40 through 55 of the book of Isaiah also had a following of disciples. Most scholars agree that some of these disciples produced chapters 56 through 66 of the book.

These verses follow the glorious climax of chapter 55, and they offer a paraphrase of Mosaic law. God asks us to prepare for salvation in justice that is about to be revealed. We must act with integrity and build justice. Foreigners are welcome. Salvation is offered to others, not just to Israel. And God's house will be a house of prayer, for all peoples.

### Responsorial Psalm: Psalm 67:2–3, 5, 6, 8

### Second Reading: Romans 11:13–15, 29–32

*God's gifts and...call are irrevocable.*

Paul describes an important motivation for him. If, by preaching the gospel to the Gentiles, he can rouse his own Jewish people to embrace their heritage, then his ministry is a source of glory. The stakes are high, including nothing less than resurrection from the dead. For Paul the lines are drawn sharply. God has proven faithful to all of Jewish tradition, in the person of Jesus, and through Jesus, God has offered salvation to the Gentiles. Jesus is the summation and climax of Jewish tradition.

Paul regards any Jewish failure to see this as an act of disobedience, a lack of fidelity to their own tradition. We can see that Paul's fond and yet hard judgment has pervaded the thinking of New Testament writers. It has influenced their language. Writing at least thirty years later than Paul, Matthew, for example, paints a mean-spirited picture of the Jews. Writing thirty or more years after Matthew, John uses language that is downright hostile. These developments are unfortunate, and they have led to tragic consequences. In light of this Pauline text, however, we can see that our most important theologian has never lost his fondness for the Jewish people. Here he even hints that it is his failure if all Jews do not embrace Jesus Christ.

God's gifts and call are irrevocable. Paul reminds first-century Christians in Rome, and us, that God called the Jewish people first, and that God has never abandoned them.

## Gospel: Matthew 15:21–28
*...you have great faith.*

Matthew portrays Jesus withdrawing to the district along the great sea (Mediterranean) following a confrontation with Pharisees and scribes. He encounters a Canaanite woman, a Gentile, who asks for his help. At first Jesus ignores her, and the disciples encourage him to dismiss her. Jesus insists that his mission is concerned with Jews only. The woman persists, and Jesus insults her with a mini-parable: It is not right to throw to dogs the food meant for children. The woman accepts this insult without flinching, and she responds that dogs are grateful for what falls off the tables of their masters. It is the prayer of a pagan, but it is not lost on Jesus. He congratulates her great faith and assures her that her wish will be fulfilled.

This passage reveals at least four things: 1. Throughout Matthew's gospel, Jesus understands his mission as being within the Jewish community. He ignores the Gentiles; 2. The woman appeals to him in the same street-smart manner in which Jesus speaks and teaches. Through this language, she exhibits a faith that surprises him; 3. The story justifies the church's mission to the Gentiles, as well as to the Jews. It manifests the power of Jesus' presence, a power not limited by national, ethnic, or religious boundaries; 4. Jesus offers the gospel to the Jews, but there is plenty left over for everyone else. God gives grace freely to all.

## Questions for Reflection

•How can you build justice? How can you organize with neighbors and friends to build justice? How does the church at large try to build justice? How can you participate in the church's ongoing efforts?

•What is your attitude toward people of other faiths, and toward the Jews in particular? How well do you respect Paul's reminder that God's gifts and call are irrevocable? How well do you live the truth that God offers grace freely, to all people?

•How do you demonstrate your faith? What do you do and say to enact what you believe?

•How do you pray? What do you ask of Jesus? What do the words you use say about your faith?

# TWENTY-FIRST SUNDAY IN ORDINARY TIME

### The Rock and building-stones

*[August 25, 1996; August 22, 1999; August 25, 2002]*

### First Reading: Isaiah 22:15, 19–23

*On that day I will summon my servant.*

An obscure figure named Shebna is to be thrust from office, and to be replaced by Eliakim, the Lord's servant. God intends to give this servant the deposed official's clothes and authority. God will place the key of the house of David on his shoulder, so that when he opens, no one will shut, and when he shuts, no one will open. This servant is to be effective. His authority will be beyond question.

This brief text is surely more significant for Christians than for Jews. The exploits of Shebna and Eliakim are long since forgotten. The prophet's powerful language, however, is echoed in Jesus' grant of authority to Peter.

### Responsorial Psalm: Psalm 138:1–2, 2–3, 6, 8

### Second Reading: Romans 11:33–36

*To him be glory forever.*

Citing Job (11:7–8; 15:8), Wisdom (9:13; 17:1), the Psalms (139:6, 17–18), Jeremiah (23:18), and the poet known to us as "second Isaiah" (40:13; 55:8–9), Paul asks rhetorical questions. Who has known the mind of the Lord? Who has been God's counselor? To whom does God owe anything? The answer to each of these questions, of course, is "No one." Drawing upon the depth and breadth of Hebrew tradition, Paul instructs Gentile Christians in Rome that God's judgments are inscrutable, God's ways unsearchable.

### Gospel: Matthew 16:13–20

*Who do you say that I am?*

After some healings, a second miraculous feeding of a crowd, and various scrapes with authorities, Jesus and the disciples arrive at Caesarea Philippi, at the headwaters of the Jordan river. Now that the disciples have seen Jesus at work for a while, he poses a question. "Who do people say that I am?" They summarize various answers: the Baptizer, Elijah, other prophets. Jesus asks a second question: "Who do you say that I am?" Simon calls him Messiah, Son of the Living God.

In reply Jesus is delighted and generous. "You are blessed, because only my Father can reveal this to you. From now on, you will be called 'Rock' [Peter], and upon this rock I shall build my church.... What you declare bound on earth is bound in heaven, and what you declare loosed on earth is loosed in heaven."

These words resemble those in the first reading. It seems odd that God would invest such power in any human being, that is, other than in Jesus. The divine trust seems almost unwarranted, in light of Eliakim's and Peter's immediate failures (see Matthew 16:21–27). Because of Peter's several failures, we must not overlook the irony in Jesus' having chosen him, nor in the name "Rock." But maybe there is hope in this very irony. If Peter is a rock at the foundation of the church, each Christian is a stone who helps to build the structure. Like Peter, each of us vacillates between insight and failure. Imperfect though we may be, we are the church, in whom Jesus has vested enormous power and authority. Sometimes effective, and sometimes in spite of ourselves, we are an enduring reality who proclaim the kingdom of God.

## Questions for Reflection

•What recent events remind you that God's ways are unsearchable, God's judgments inscrutable? If we cannot know God's mind, how can we know how to act? Why would you believe in our unknowable God, instead of a smaller, easier, more predictable pagan "god"?

•Who do people say that Jesus is? Who do you say that Jesus is, deep in your heart of hearts? How does your answer compare or contrast with Peter's?

•What are the church's strengths? What are the church's weaknesses? What signs suggest that we do continue to proclaim the gospel in a broken world? How can we improve? What can you do to make the church more effective and credible?

# TWENTY-SECOND SUNDAY IN ORDINARY TIME

*Take up your cross*

[September 1, 1996; August 29, 1999; September 1, 2002]

### First Reading: Jeremiah 20:7–9

*The word of the Lord has brought me derision.*

Known throughout the land for his bold condemnations of political and religious foolishness, Jeremiah pays repeatedly for his outcries. Scourged and placed in stocks, the prophet in these verses reflects on his relationship with God's word. He offers a bitter complaint: "You duped me, Lord, and now I am a laughingstock. I have no choice but to speak out in outrage, but for my troubles I have earned derision and reproach. If I try to remain silent, the word of the Lord becomes like a fire burning in my heart, imprisoned in my bones. I cannot stand to hold it in."

### Responsorial Psalm: Psalm 63:2, 3–4, 5–6, 8–9

### Second Reading: Romans 12:1–2

*Be transformed by the renewal of your minds.*

Paul appeals to his Roman audience: "Offer your bodies as living sacrifice, as spiritual worship. Do not conform to this age, but be transformed, in order to discern and to do God's will."

These words are useful for us as well. As the pope has reminded us, we are to be a "sign of contradiction," a prophetic challenge to our age. But we should not make the mistake of merely being contrary. There is little virtue in disagreeing with everything, while standing for nothing. Recall that Paul's theology is built upon an understanding of the Spirit giving life and value to inert matter. If we regard our bodies as sacrifices, as Christ regarded his own human body, we will allow the Spirit to guide us. Then we may do what is pleasing, maybe even perfect.

### Gospel: Matthew 16:21–27

*Get out of my sight, you Satan!*

Peter the Rock is the first to call Jesus "Messiah" (Matthew 16:13–30,

21st Sunday in ordinary time). He is also the first to misunderstand what this discovery means. Now that Peter and the others recognize him as Messiah, Jesus begins to speak of going to Jerusalem, where he will be killed and raised up. Peter takes Jesus aside to try to talk him out of this crazy plan. Jesus' response is swift and devastating. "You are an agent of Satan, the trickster. You are a stumbling-stone, trying to trip me."

Then Jesus states the ironic and central invitation of the Christian way. To follow me, he says, you must deny yourself, take up your cross, walk in my footsteps. If you lose your life for my sake, you will find life. If you cling to life, you will lose it. At the end, when I return, I will repay everyone according to his or her conduct.

Through this episode and the one immediately preceding it, we should not overlook Peter's pattern of conduct. Upon naming Jesus "Messiah," Peter receives the Lord's most enthusiastic and generous blessing. But here, a mere six verses further on in Matthew's narrative, he has earned Jesus' most scathing condemnation. Nowhere else in the gospel accounts does Jesus use such strong language.

We must understand that our discoveries and faith do not necessarily make things easier for us. In fact, the truth is quite the opposite. If we are able to call upon Jesus as Christ-Savior-Messiah, God expects far more from us than if we could not profess faith in this way. And there is no way around it. Our faith leads to and through the cross. Like Peter, we are gifted with occasional insights, and sometimes we fail. But also like Peter, we have no excuses. Like Jeremiah, we have no choice. We must speak out for the sake of, and act upon, the word of God.

## Questions for Reflection

•When have you felt that you must speak out about something? When did you hold something inside, feeling as though you were going to burst? When, if ever, did God's word demand that you speak out?

•When were you first able to recognize Jesus as savior and lord? How has your life changed since that time? What has gotten easier for you? What has grown more difficult?

•How do you like the thought of being a living sacrifice? What is your cross? What do you have to do to pick it up and follow Jesus?

# TWENTY-THIRD SUNDAY IN ORDINARY TIME

*Our responsibilities for others*

*[September 8, 1996; September 5, 1999; September 8, 2002]*

### First Reading: Ezekiel 33:7–9

*I have appointed [you] watchman....*

In these verses the prophet is compared to a sentinel in a watchtower. By virtue of a location far above the city, the sentinel can see things that escape everyone else's notice. His or her job is to warn everyone about impending attack. If the sentinel fails to give proper warning, he or she is held responsible for any fate that befalls the city.

This text tells us that God has appointed Ezekiel as watchman, or sentinel, for the house of Israel. Graced with God-given insight and judgment, the prophet must sound warnings, trying to persuade the wicked to change their ways. If the prophet fails in this duty, he is held responsible for the fates of those he should have warned. Today, in a different time and a different place, we Christians are also called to be responsible for others.

### Responsorial Psalm: Psalm 95:1–2, 6–7, 8–9

### Second Reading: Romans 13:8–10

*...love is the fulfillment of the law.*

In the middle of an examination of authority, taxes, and good Christian citizenship, Paul speaks about debts. The only appropriate debt is the one that binds Christians to love one another. All other debts should be paid off, and no new ones incurred. More important, he insists that all the commandments may be summed up in this statement: Love your neighbor as yourself. Since love never does any wrong to the neighbor, it is the fulfillment of the law.

Talk like this is not a Christian innovation. Many Jewish teachers of Paul's and Jesus' time also insisted that Leviticus 19:18 and Deuteronomy 6:4–5 could be read as summaries of the entire law. It is possible, but not certain, that early Christians thought of the term "neighbor" in a broader sense than did other Jewish teachers, and maybe in a universal sense. But in this instance Paul, like Jesus, echoes a widespread Jewish teaching.

## Gospel: Matthew 18:15–20

*...there I am in the midst of them.*

In this text about authority and conduct in the local church, Jesus teaches the disciples a procedure for dealing with grievances. First, the one who has been harmed should confront the offender directly. If a one-on-one confrontation does not work, the aggrieved party should talk to the offender again, but this time in the presence of one or two witnesses. If this second step does not work, the local church should hold a public consultation among all its members. If at last nothing works, the church should treat the offender like a Gentile or tax collector, which means excommunication for the offender.

Jesus also seems to give the disciples impressive authority: "What you bind on earth is bound in heaven, and what you 'loose' on earth is 'loosed' in heaven." And there is more. When two or more disciples agree about something for which to pray, the Father grants it.

Like Ezekiel, we Christians bear responsibility to speak against sin and error. We exercise this responsibility as church when we gather in unity, when Christ is among us.

## Questions for Reflection

•How do you settle grievances or misunderstandings? How do you correct someone if you think he or she is in the wrong? How do these texts challenge or reinforce your behavior?

•If love fulfills the law, how does your knowledge of God's commandments enrich your understanding of what love is?

•What sorts of actions express love? What kinds of actions must Christians avoid? How can you be relatively sure that God approves of your choices and actions?

# TWENTY-FOURTH SUNDAY IN ORDINARY TIME

*Forgiveness, gratitude, and responsibility*

[September 15, 1996; September 12, 1999; September 15, 2002]

### First Reading: Sirach 27:30–28:7

*Forgive your neighbor's injustice....*

Among Sirach's long collection of observations about life, we find today's verses on anger, sin, vengeance, and forgiveness. The sinner clings to anger, the vengeful will feel the Lord's vengeance. In a precursor to Jesus' own prayer, Sirach insists that when we forgive the neighbor's injustice our own sins will be forgiven.

It is essential that the person of faith keep the reality of death in mind and stop sinning. He or she must remember the commandments, as well as the covenant to which each Christian is bound. Sirach implies that life is too short to be filled up with hate and anger.

### Responsorial Psalm: Psalm 103:1–2, 3–4, 9–10, 11–12

### Second Reading: Romans 14:7–9

*Both in life and in death we are the Lord's.*

Throughout this letter, Paul responds to disagreements among the Christians in Rome. He intends to settle their arguments by appealing to basic tenets of faith. Yet his responses speak to all Christians, in all times.

In this text he makes the point that whatever choices we face, we are not our own masters. In life and in death we are the Lord's servants. Indeed, Christ died and came into new life in order that he might be lord of everyone who lives, as well as lord of everyone who has died.

### Gospel: Matthew 18:21–35

*My heavenly Father will treat you in exactly the same way.*

When Peter asks Jesus how often he should forgive someone who wrongs him, Jesus insists that he must forgive "seventy times seven" times. Then he summarizes the proper behavior of the individual disciple, and of the church, with a parable in three scenes.

In the first scene a king intends to settle accounts with his officials. One owes an enormous amount, and as he cannot pay, the king orders him to be sold, along with family and property, to repay the debt. But the man begs for patience, promising to pay back everything, in full. In response, the king does more than he has been asked, canceling the debt.

In scene two, the same official demands payment from one of his own debtors. When the man begs for mercy, he refuses to hear of it, and throws the man in jail. But the king hears of this incident, and in the final scene the king brings the official in before him to condemn his actions. To conclude, Jesus assures Peter that his heavenly Father will treat him in exactly this manner unless he forgives brother and sister from the heart. The implication is clear. The Father has already forgiven each of us many more debts than we can ever imagine. We must act toward others in a manner like that which has been granted to us.

This story illustrates graphically the phrase in the Lord's prayer, "Forgive us, as we forgive." It also suggests the enormity of the gifts with which God has blessed us. We are like the heavily-indebted servant, and we have asked God to reschedule our payments. Acting as only God can do, God has canceled the debt. The next move is ours.

## Questions for Reflection

•What makes you angry? How do you deal with your anger? When can anger be a good thing? When and how can you use anger productively or creatively? What are some destructive ways of expressing anger?

•How easy is it for you to forgive someone? What kinds of things tend to prevent you from offering forgiveness more readily than you do?

•The parable portrays God as a gracious king who forgives debts and who demands that we act with similar generosity. How does this portrait compare with your notion of God? How do you have to adjust your portrait? What does the parable tell you about the grace already given to you? How does it challenge your actions? How does it affirm your behavior?

# TWENTY-FIFTH SUNDAY IN ORDINARY TIME

*God's fairness*

[September 22, 1996; September 19, 1999; September 22, 2002]

### First Reading: Isaiah 55:6–9

*For my thoughts are not your thoughts...*

Chapter 55 of Isaiah contains the climax and conclusion of the work of "second Isaiah," who wrote two centuries after Isaiah's death. This text comes from the middle of the chapter, in which it functions as a pivot. The first two verses conclude the invitation extended in the chapter's first half, and the latter verses bring description and promise.

"Seek the Lord," goes the invitation, "Call upon God while God is near." The scoundrels and the wicked are invited to change their ways, to turn to God, who is always merciful and generous in forgiveness.

People can change, says the poet, because God's ways are not our ways; God's thoughts are not our thoughts. Although God is near, God's ways of thinking and acting are as far above our ways as the heavens are above the earth.

### Responsorial Psalm: Psalm 145:2–3, 8–9, 17–18

### Second Reading: Philippians 1:20–24, 27

*Christ will be exalted through me, whether I live or die.*

Writing from prison, Paul exhibits a saint's detachment from his fate. This is not to say that he does not care whether he lives or dies. He has, however, focused his gaze on a higher purpose. Whatever happens to him, Christ will be exalted. If he dies, he gains eternal union with Christ. If he is allowed to live, he can continue to work among people on Christ's behalf.

Paul tells his disciples that he does not know which to prefer, and that he is at peace with whatever comes. A concluding verse urges the audience to live in a way worthy of the gospel.

### Gospel: Matthew 20:1–16

*...the last shall be first and the first shall be last.*

In this parable Jesus compares the kingdom of God to the case of an estate owner who hired workers at different hours of the day. Some began working at dawn, others at mid-morning, still others at noon, and others at mid-afternoon. Yet all received the same wage, a full day's pay. The workers who had started at daybreak felt that they deserved more than people who had only worked for an hour. The owner replied to one, "My friend, I do you no injustice." After all, everyone had agreed upon the same wage. Concluding, Jesus says, "The last shall be first and the first shall be last."

From the beginning this story has been certain to offend Jewish audiences, with its suggestion that latecomers could share their inheritance via Christian belief. Even apart from first-century church and synagogue disputes, however, this story seems calculated to offend. By any human standard of fairness, those who work all day are right to expect more than others who work shorter shifts. But as the first reading insists, God's ways are not our ways. God gives with a generosity that exceeds anything we can give. Sometimes in our little minds, we think God's grace is unfair.

### Questions for Reflection

•What recent experience reminds you of the difference between your ways and God's ways?

•What do you like about Jesus' story of the workers in the vineyard? What do you dislike? How does the story challenge you?

•How and when have you been graced by God's "unfair" generosity?

# TWENTY-SIXTH SUNDAY IN ORDINARY TIME

*Real obedience*

*[September 29, 1996; September 26, 1999; September 29, 2002]*

### First Reading: Ezekiel 18:25–28

*Is it my way that is unfair?...*

The readings raise questions of fairness and God's action, as do the readings of the 25th Sunday in ordinary time, year A. Ezekiel speaks on God's behalf, challenging the house of Israel: "Who is really unfair here? Is it I or is it you? If a good man turns to sin, he must die because of his sin. But if a sinner shapes up and does what is right and just, then the reformed sinner will live." What seems to matter more than anything else is the general direction of a person's life. If we move from bad to good, God is pleased, but God is quite unhappy if we move in the opposite direction. Our choices do matter.

### Responsorial Psalm: Psalm 125:4–5, 6–7, 8–9

### Second Reading: Philippians 2:1–11

*Rather, he emptied himself....*

In the first five verses of this text, Paul encourages the audience to live and act united in spirit and ideals. Rivalry and conceit are out of the question. Instead, each person must place the interests of others ahead of his or her own. The Christian must develop an attitude that is Christ's.

The remaining six verses are composed of a hymn that seems to have existed earlier than this letter, and that may have been sung at liturgies throughout the primitive Christian world, right from the start. It is notable for its cadences, for its use of parallelism, and for its vocabulary, which differs from that of the rest of the letter. These verses also comprise our epistle reading each year at Passion (Palm) Sunday.

The hymn sketches our most basic beliefs. Its first half insists that Christ is God's equal, but that nevertheless he emptied himself, having been born in our likeness. As one of us, he accepted everything that came his way, even death on the cross. The second half of the hymn describes Christ's exaltation, and tells of his place in the universe. Every knee must bend (before him) and every tongue proclaim, Jesus Christ is lord!

While not everyone is required to suffer the total abasement of the cross, each Christian must yet be prepared to follow Christ all the way, even to the cross. That is the essential ingredient in our faith, if we are to live together and meet our responsibilities.

### Gospel: Matthew 21:28–32
*Which of the two did what the father wanted?*

Having arrived in Jerusalem, Jesus has been challenged by the high priests and elders concerning the authority upon which his teaching rests. He has silenced them in front of witnesses, and now he poses a choice. A man with two sons asks them to work in the vineyard. The elder agrees to go, but he never does. The younger refuses the father's request, but later in the day he regrets this response and works in the vineyard. "Which son did the father's will?" asks Jesus. The priests and elders reply that the second son has acted properly. Then, in a move guaranteed to win him powerful enemies, Jesus assures them that tax collectors and prostitutes are entering the kingdom of God before them. He also implies that Gentiles will earn God's reward before many of the Jews.

Encounters like this seal Jesus' fate. There is a deeper challenge for us, however, beneath the historical narrative that makes Jesus' crucifixion inevitable. Actions are more important than words. Doing God's will is much better than talking about God's will. What seems most important, however, is the general movement of our lives. Do our choices lead us ever more closely to live God's will? That is the essential question which describes a movement that God rewards with God's unique brand of fairness.

### Questions for Reflection

•Think of significant choices you have made during the past year. What pattern do they suggest? In which direction are you moving?

•How do you or will you express an attitude like Christ's? What must you continue to do? What must you change?

•What promises have you made to God? Which have you kept? Which remain unfulfilled? What must you do to fulfill them?

# TWENTY-SEVENTH SUNDAY IN ORDINARY TIME

*Vineyards and their fruit*

[October 6, 1996; October 3, 1999; October 6, 2002]

### First Reading: Isaiah 5:1–7
*My friend had a vineyard....*

All of Jesus' vineyard parables are built upon this text, Isaiah's "song of the vineyard." This poem is itself a parable, a narrative with an unexpected twist that illustrates an aspect of God's truth. Moreover, it may be Isaiah's most important prophecy, for it is marvelous poetry and it reveals the logic of prophecy as well as any text can do.

"My friend," sings the prophet, "created a vineyard and gave it every advantage, and expected it to yield fine wine. Instead it produced wild grapes [literally 'rotten, stinking fruit']. Judge between me and my vineyard: Who is responsible for the wild grapes? I will flatten the vineyard and I [God] will command the rain to avoid it. By the way, Israel, you are the vineyard. God seeks your ethical example, but you continue to spill blood. God demands justice, and yet God continues to hear the outcry of the weak who are trampled by the strong."

After telling the whole story in the first two verses, the poet appeals to the judgment of the audience, absolutely certain of the answer. This is a classic prophetic device (see also 2 Samuel 12:1–15, especially verses 5 and 6; 1 Kings 21, especially verses 17–21; and Amos 1:3–2:16, especially 2:6–16). In verses 5 and 6 the owner declares the fate of the vineyard, and the last verse is the clincher: "You are the vineyard."

Appealing to the audience's powers of observation and common sense, the poet has delivered a message that reveals a truth. In this case, it is an unwelcome truth, but a truth nonetheless. When Jesus speaks in parables, he stands within the tradition of the great prophets.

### Responsorial Psalm: Psalm 80:9, 12, 13–14, 15–16, 19–20

### Second Reading: Philippians 4:6–9
*Live according to what you have learned and accepted.*

Nearing the end of his letter from prison, Paul encourages the church at Philippi to dismiss anxiety and to pray, so that God's peace will stand guard over them. He urges them to direct their thoughts to what he has taught them. Paul's words assure Jesus' followers that if they empty themselves of anxiety, they will be filled with what is honest, pure, admirable, virtuous, and true.

## Gospel: Matthew 21:33–43
*...he leased it out to tenant farmers....*

Jesus poses another question for the chief priests and elders in Jerusalem. The story this time bears a striking resemblance to Isaiah's song of the vineyard. But in Matthew's version of Jesus' reinterpretation of the story, the owner leases out the vineyard to tenant farmers. Absent at vintage time, he sends servants to obtain his share, but the tenants beat some and kill others. A second round of servants receives the same treatment. Finally, the owner sends his son, whom the tenants drag outside and kill. "Now what will the owner do to those tenants?" asks Jesus. The reply is that he will destroy them and lease the property to other tenants.

Jesus then refers to Psalm 118:22–23, about the rejected stone that becomes the cornerstone, and he delivers his closing statement: "The kingdom of God will be taken from you and given to those who will yield a rich harvest."

What is most important for us here is the story's enduring revolutionary character. Membership in a religion guarantees nothing. Catholics today can no more afford to be smug than could their first-century privileged and chosen counterparts in Jerusalem. What matters is that we who tend the Lord's vineyard respect Son and servants, and give to God, the owner, a rightful portion of the fruits of our labors.

## Questions for Reflection

•Imagine that you are a vine in God's vineyard. How have you been tended? What advantages have been given to you, and what have been withheld from you?

•What has God expected from you? What have you produced?

•What does God expect from the church, which is made up of many individual Christians and groups of individuals? What have your groups of friends produced? What has your parish produced?

# TWENTY-EIGHTH SUNDAY IN ORDINARY TIME

*God's banquet*

[October 13, 1996; October 10, 1999; October 13, 2002]

### First Reading: Isaiah 25:6–10

*...he will destroy death forever.*

In Isaiah's thinking, the God of Israel is the God of all peoples. This text promises a feast for everyone. It is to be a feast more sumptuous than we can imagine, and an occasion of unity and celebration for all. The veil of death will be lifted from everyone. The reproach of God's people will be erased, for God's word has the power to do this. All nations will join in a joyful hymn thanking God for salvation. All these things will take place on top of a mountain, upon which God's hand will rest. All nations will share the divine favor granted to Israel.

### Responsorial Psalm: Psalm 23:1–3, 3–4, 5, 6

### Philippians 4:12–14, 19–20

*My God in turn will supply your needs fully....*

Paul continues to display his detachment from everything that is not essential. For him, the only essential is the gospel. In this text, he expresses his gratitude for the local church's willingness to understand and to empathize with his hardships. Even so, in so many words he says politely, "Thanks, but no thanks." He has learned that his real needs will always be met. He remains indifferent to both hardship and bounty. He offers his own kind of blessing: "As my needs have been met, God will give you everything you need. Glory to God, Amen."

This text can help us to appreciate the difference between our needs and our wants. If we examine all our motives (our wants, needs, habits, biases, everything), eventually we discover the deepest motive of all, a passion to love and serve God. This passion underlies Paul's response to the Philippians' expression of concern. For Paul, and in every subsequent expression of true Christian teaching, the passion to love and serve God is the deepest motive of each human person. It is what defines us.

## Gospel: Matthew 22:1–14

*The banquet is ready....*

This parable refers to the feast described in the first reading, Isaiah 25:6–10. The kingdom of God is like a wedding banquet given by a king for his son. Twice the king sends servants to invite guests, but not only is the invitation refused, many of the servants are killed. The enraged king destroys the original invitees and directs the servants to summon anyone and everyone to come to the banquet. Finally, when the hall is filled, the king ejects someone who is not properly dressed. He explains this action: "Many are called, but few are the elect."

This is the last parable that Jesus presents to the chief priests and elders in Matthew's account of the gospel. It is surely not intended to make friends. The original invitees are some of the chosen people, those who have failed to accept God's invitation. After they have been punished for their lack of faith, the whole world is invited. In a sense, this new invitation is like the dragnet (Matthew 13:44–52, 17th Sunday in ordinary time, year A). Everyone is pulled in, but only the elect, here those dressed properly, perhaps in baptismal clothes, can stay at the table. On the other hand, anyone who is hauled in by God's invitation, yet continues to frustrate God's will, will be ejected.

Like the chief priests and elders, we are the targets of this biting parable. We have been hauled into the kingdom by virtue of God's overwhelming generosity. But having once seen what the kingdom is like, we cannot just do any old thing. We must conduct ourselves in ways that allow us to stay at the table. The mere fact that we call ourselves Christians is not enough, we must also act like Christians. If our baptisms have become empty, forgotten rituals, they do us no good. Everyone is called to the kingdom. But coming into the kingdom is one thing, staying there is quite another. The Christian must be prepared to follow Christ to the cross.

### Questions for Reflection

•What aspects of life will be destroyed or cease to exist at the Lord's banquet? What positive things will fill the world? What promising signs do you see in our world today?

•How do you deal with hardship? How does your response to hardship compare with that of Paul? How can you improve in this area? Whose help do you need? What resources and activities will help you?

•What would you have to do to be properly "dressed" for the wedding feast? What are you already doing well? What changes must you make?

# TWENTY-NINTH SUNDAY IN ORDINARY TIME

## God's likeness

*[October 20, 1996; October 17, 1999; October 20, 2002]*

### First Reading: Isaiah 45:1, 4–6

*I have called you by your name....*

During a seventy-year exile in Babylon, in the sixth century before Jesus, the people of Abraham and David gave shape to their Scriptures, their liturgical life, their Jewishness. Toward the end of that century, Cyrus the Persian gained power sufficient to topple the Babylonian empire. More important, he permitted the Jews to return to their homeland (see 2 Chronicles 36:22–23, 4th Sunday in Lent, year B, and Ezra 1:1–3).

For the anonymous poet whose work is inserted into the book of Isaiah, Cyrus is a hero. God has seized Cyrus' right hand, to open gates for the sake of God's chosen people. Although he does not know God, Cyrus is God's instrument who liberates the Jews so that, ultimately, all the world may know God.

### Responsorial Psalm: Psalm 96:1, 3, 4–5, 7–8, 9–10

### Second Reading: 1 Thessalonians 1:1–5

*We keep thanking God for all of you....*

These verses are probably the earliest writing in the New Testament. Their tone is upbeat, overflowing with praise for the Thessalonica church's witness of the gospel. Writing on behalf of companions Silvanus and Timothy, Paul offers grace and peace to the audience. He is grateful for their faith, for their charitable work, for their constancy in hope. Most important, he notes their complete conviction, which finds expression in more than mere words.

In this earliest written reference to the term "gospel," we find an important clue to all of Paul's thought. The gospel is both word and deed, a word that demands action. Anyone who mouths the words of the gospel without also enacting it distorts it beyond recognition. That is why Paul is so enthusiastic in his praise for the church at Thessalonica. The gospel is not mere words for them, but power. He reminds them, and us, of the very high standard to which Christians aspire.

## Gospel: Matthew 22:15–21
*...give to God what is God's.*

The confrontation in Jerusalem continues. Having shamed and embarrassed officials with a series of challenging parables, here Jesus faces disciples of Pharisees, and Herodian sympathizers. They have plotted to trap him in speech, and they ask him, "Is it lawful to pay taxes to the emperor or not?" It is a clever question. To answer in the affirmative is to pledge allegiance to a foreign king with divine pretensions. No self-respecting Jewish teacher could do such a thing. To answer "No" is to take a public stance guaranteed to bring the weight of the occupying Roman empire on his head. But Jesus sees through their trap and asks them whose likeness appears on the coins of commerce and taxation. They identify Caesar's coin, and he teaches, "Give to Caesar what is Caesar's and to God what belongs to God." And where is God's likeness? This episode only implies an answer, but we know it, as do those who have confronted Jesus. God's imprint is upon every human face. We are the image of God. We must give to God what is God's. We must give to God everything that matters in ourselves.

This story condones neither civil disobedience nor complete acquiescence to the requirements of the state. It is about neither. Instead, it forces us to look deep within ourselves and ask what we really do give to God. Jesus escapes the trap set for him by insisting that we must direct our entire selves to the Creator whose likeness we bear.

## Questions for Reflection

•How can someone who is not a believer do God's work? What does the example of Cyrus suggest? What examples can you identify in our modern world? Who seems to be doing God's work, in fact if not in name?

•How easy would it be for an observer to hear the gospel in your words? How clearly is the gospel visible in your actions? How do your words and actions distort the gospel? How believably do you live what you say and say what you live?

•How do you balance your obligations to God and state? How often do you encounter conflicts between the two? How do you resolve these conflicts? What other obligations sometimes conflict with what is due to God? How do you resolve these conflicts? What changes should you make, if any?

# THIRTIETH SUNDAY
# IN ORDINARY TIME
## Love God, love your neighbor
*[October 27, 1996; October 24, 1999; October 27, 2002]*

### First Reading: Exodus 22:20–26
*...I am compassionate.*

The law of Moses consists of many different kinds of mandates scattered through the books we know as Exodus, Leviticus, Numbers, and Deuteronomy. Embedded in historical narrative, the law cannot be forced to stand alone as some kind of code or rule book. It only makes sense within the historical relationship between a people and their God.

This text illustrates the first principle underlying all of Israel's life: God is compassionate, and the people must act as their God acts. God tells Moses what to teach Israel: "You were aliens not long ago, so you must not oppress the alien. You shall not harm a widow or an orphan. When you lend money, do it honestly, and return promptly anything you borrow." In the law, God gives the Hebrews, and us, a pattern for compassionate behavior.

### Responsorial Psalm: Psalm 18:2–3, 3–4, 47, 51

### Second Reading: 1 Thessalonians 1:5–10
*The word of the Lord has echoed forth from you....*

Paul continues to praise his audience. "You became models for all the believers in your area by turning to God from idols, and by serving Jesus," he says. "The word of the Lord has echoed forth from you re-soundingly." The church in Thessalonica is an example of the gospel proclaimed and lived. It invites us to examine the kind of example we set today.

### Gospel: Matthew 22:34–40
*You shall love the Lord your God....*

Jesus has exposed the hypocrisy of chief priests and elders with parables (Matthew 21:28–32; 33–43; 22:1–14). In front of admiring crowds, Jesus has shown that the "authorities," the caste of priests and guardians of the temple, have failed to understand the Scriptures. He has also eluded the trap of Pharisees and Herodians with the question of Caesar's coin (Matthew 22:15–21; see the 26th–29th Sundays in ordinary time, year A).

In this text the Pharisees have regrouped, and a lawyer from among them tests Jesus with a question. "Which is the greatest commandment?" Jesus responds, quoting Deuteronomy 6:5: "Love your God." This verse is a summary of the first three of the familiar ten commandments. Jesus then says that the second commandment is like the first, "You shall love your neighbor as yourself." This statement, too, is a quotation, of Leviticus 19:18. Jesus uses it here to summarize all those commandments that describe proper relations among human persons.

The two commandments belong together. Love of God and love of neighbor are inseparable. We express our love in concrete terms, never merely in words. If we love God, we enact God's own compassion in our dealings with others. For Jesus, as for Paul and for those ancient and unknown editors who compiled the Torah, this ethical standard is the real substance of the law. Confronted by Pharisees who may be friendly even as they contest his thinking, Jesus names these two commandments in the same breath. He answers the test question with the heart and foundation of the Mosaic law. In this manner, he also invites us into a way of life.

## Questions for Reflection

•What are the many ways in which God has acted with compassion in history? How does God act in compassion in our world? How has God's compassion touched you?

•What would you have to do for Paul to say of you, "The word of the Lord has echoed forth from you resoundingly"? What would the group of Christians with whom you are associated most closely have to do for Paul to respond to you in this way? What would your parish have to do?

•How well do you love your neighbor as yourself? What concrete evidence helps you to know how good a job you are doing? How do you fail to love your neighbor? How often do you make excuses to justify behavior that is easy for you, or that benefits you? How well do you love your God?

# THIRTY-FIRST SUNDAY IN ORDINARY TIME

*Authentic leadership*

*[November 3, 1996; October 31, 1999; November 3, 2002]*

### First Reading: Malachi 1:14–2:2, 8–10

*Have we not all the one Father?*

The short book of Malachi castigates the priestly class and laypersons alike for their sins against God. In introducing the figure of the messenger of the covenant, it also warns the audience of impending doom for all but the righteous few.

These verses represent the book's sense of menace. It scolds the priests for failing as teachers, for causing many to falter by their instruction. They have voided the ancient priestly covenant by showing partiality in their decisions and, in unspecified ways, by departing from the basic doctrine of the law, which insists that there is one God.

In this view of things, good teaching is always honest. To walk with God in integrity and in uprightness is to turn others away from evil. The good leader or teacher inspires by example, embodying in his or her person the very words that he or she speaks.

### Responsorial Psalm: Psalm 131:1, 2, 3

### Second Reading: 1 Thessalonians 2:7–9, 13

*...we were as gentle as any nursing mother.*

Paul is terribly fond of the Christians whom he addresses in what is probably his oldest surviving letter. He has called them model Christians and resounding echoes of God's word. Here he compares his affection for them to that of a mother fondling her babies. He has wanted to share his very life with these Christians. But most of all he is grateful that they have received his teaching for what it is, the word of God at work within them.

### Gospel: Matthew 23:1–12

*Whoever exalts himself shall be humbled,*
*but whoever humbles himself shall be exalted.*

Jesus lashes out at the Pharisees and scribes in a tone and with a message similar to Malachi's: The recognized leaders speak the right words, but that is where it ends. Jesus recognizes authentic teaching, and he could hardly speak more plainly. The scribes and the Pharisees have succeeded Moses as teachers. His audience must do what these authorities say, because their words are authentic. Their examples, however, are thoroughly bankrupt. Their actions brand them as hypocrites. They seem most interested in titles, honors, and sitting in places of respect.

Jesus also instructs the crowd and his disciples that they must call no one "father" or "teacher." Painful experience reminds many Catholics today how often some people who call themselves Christian use Matthew 23:9 to challenge us on the way we address our priests. They miss the point. This verse is not a law about titles. It is something much deeper. Here Jesus teaches everyone that there is but one father of us all, and our one teacher is the Messiah, the one who has become servant of all. The way to glory leads through a humility that echoes Jesus' own. When we follow Jesus to the cross, we live and teach with real authority.

## Questions for Reflection

•How often do you demand to be treated with respect? By contrast, how often do you really try to serve others?

•If there is only one teacher, what are we, the rest of us? What does this central truth suggest about the ways in which teaching tends to be done in church and society? Where and how does a teacher claim the right to teach? How, and on what basis, can anyone presume to lead others, either in church or in society?

•If we are all children of the same father, who are your brothers and sisters? How can this truth change the ways in which you think about and act toward others?

# THIRTY-SECOND SUNDAY IN ORDINARY TIME

*Seek wisdom*

*[November 10, 1996; November 7, 1999; November 10, 2002]*

### First Reading: Wisdom 6:12–16

*Resplendent and unfading is Wisdom.*

In the two or three centuries before Jesus' birth, centers of Jewish learning were scattered throughout the Mediterranean world. Some lectures and textbooks used in these centers have been included in our Bible. Their insights often illuminate beliefs expressed later by Christians.

This text speaks of Wisdom as person. She is resplendent and unfading. She is found readily by all who seek her. For her part, Wisdom is eager to make herself known to all. She sits by the gate of everyone's metaphorical home. The most prudent thing one can do is to think of Wisdom, because she makes her rounds and appears to all who seek her.

### Responsorial Psalm: Psalm 63:2, 3–4, 5–6, 7–8

### Second Reading: 1 Thessalonians 4:13–18

*The Lord himself will come down from heaven.*

Superficially, these verses seem to support talk about a "rapture": The Lord will come, accompanied by angelic trumpets, to meet the righteous and the re-animated deceased in mid-air. Some Christians, even some entire denominations, have built their lives upon this and similar texts. In doing so, they too often neglect what really is most important.

Jesus Christ's Easter has already occurred, and it can transform our lives today and forever. Most tragically, in their mistaken emphasis on what has not yet occurred, some folks profess a judgmental, self-righteous message that tends to isolate Christians from society and the world.

Yes, Christians must anticipate the Lord, who will surely come to us again one day. We must also act toward one another in ways that build justice and peace, in ways that resemble Christ's own love for us. Our belief in a second coming can never justify conduct that fails to resemble Christ's own example. Easter has made Christian life possible and credible, and has given us hope for the Lord's return.

### Gospel: Matthew 25:1–13

*Keep your eyes open....*

In a parable, Jesus teaches the disciples about the reign of God. It can be likened to bridesmaids who take torches to welcome the groom. Five take spare oil with their lamps, while five take only lamps. Very late, the groom is spotted as he approaches. The bridesmaids are awakened, but by this time half of them have burned all the oil for their lamps. They ask the others to share, but they are told that there may not be enough. So the five bridesmaids who failed to plan ahead must leave to buy more oil. Meanwhile, the groom arrives, the feast begins, and the door is barred. Jesus concludes with a moral: "Keep your eyes open, for you do not know the day or the hour."

This parable holds a message similar to the one found in Matthew 13:47–50 (17th Sunday in ordinary time, year A), in which fisherpeople throw out a dragnet and catch all kinds of fish, both good and bad, along with seaweed and junk from the bottom of the lake. In both stories the reign of God embraces everyone, but not everyone will be allowed to stay in God's kingdom. Here the five bridesmaids are caught unprepared, and they miss the groom's coming, as well as the wedding feast. When they beg to be allowed in, it is too late.

This story works on two levels. It reports the historical fact that some have recognized Jesus as God's Son. It also anticipates the Lord's return, the subject of the epistle reading. On both levels, the story amplifies the point of Wisdom 6:12–16, the first reading. Keep yourself ready at all times. God is near, more near than we can imagine, and we must be prepared to receive God.

### Questions for Reflection

•Who is wise? Whom do you know who is wise? Who are other wise persons in the world? What is it about them that allows you to call them wise?

•Why is Christ's Easter the pivotal event in history? Why would it be a mistake to neglect Easter while giving extra attention to an anticipated second coming? How does Easter oblige us? What are we responsible to do, until the Lord returns?

•What sort of bridesmaid would you have been in this gospel story? How well-prepared are you to meet the Lord? What must you do to prepare yourself more adequately?

# THIRTY-THIRD SUNDAY IN ORDINARY TIME

## Gifts

*[November 17, 1996; November 14, 1999; November 17, 2002]*

### First Reading: Proverbs 31:10–13, 19–20, 30–31

*...let her works praise her at the city gates.*

Only in a culture given shape by males could it seem appropriate to list the attributes of a worthy wife. Even so, these verses from the conclusion of the book of Proverbs praise a woman for her initiative, her intelligence, and for her civic and social responsibility. She manages a household, but she also earns wages with the works of her hands and her mind. Hardly an appendage to someone else, she has earned a reputation by her care for the poor and the needy. The husband entrusts his heart to her, and she is clearly his equal. She portrays the heart of the ancient covenant, acting for justice and always in awe of the Lord. As this ancient and yet enlightened portrait reveals, she is an example for all people today.

### Responsorial Psalm: Psalm 128:1–2, 3, 4–5

### Second Reading: 1 Thessalonians 5:1–6

*...the day of the Lord is coming like a thief in the night.*

Paul continues to speak urgently of the Lord's return. Since no one can know specifics about time and place, we should prepare for the Lord to come when least expected, as a thief in the night. In other words, we must always be ready, even when we are most relaxed. Anyone claiming peace and security will meet ruin as painful and as sudden as labor, and from which there will be no escape, and through which a new life begins. Christians are children of light. We have no excuses for inattention. We must remain awake and sober.

### Gospel: Matthew 25:14–30

*You are an industrious and reliable servant.*

Jesus tells a parable about a man entrusting portions of his funds to three servants. One receives five thousand silver pieces, another receives two thousand, and the last receives one thousand. When the master leaves, two servants invest their money, while the other buries his share. The master returns to find that each of the first two servants has doubled the money placed in his care. "Well done," says the master to each. "Come, share your master's joy!" But the third servant returns the original sum, citing fear of the master to justify his inaction. Enraged, the master pronounces the man lazy and worthless: "You know that I reap where I did not sow, and yet you did nothing to gain a bigger harvest for me." Then he strips the servant of all responsibility and tosses him out to the darkness where he can wail and grind his teeth.

A master-servant parable always teaches us something about our relationships with God. Most people can appreciate the initiative of the two servants who invest the funds entrusted to them and who double their master's money. But what about the other servant? Most of us know fear, and the temptation of inaction or paralysis that sometimes comes with it. The servant's punishment seems unduly harsh, especially in light of Jesus' pronouncement that those who have will gain while those who lack will lose. It is hard to square this teaching with our belief in an all-merciful God.

Yet there is no compromise. Each of us is given a share of God's gifts, and God really does reap where God has not sown. This parable insists that when the master returns to settle accounts with us, he will expect us to have multiplied our gifts. We have no choice but to do something creative, life-giving, and just with the gifts entrusted to us.

## Questions for Reflection

•How important does care for the poor and needy appear to be, throughout the Bible? Where is care for the poor and needy among your many priorities?

•In the first reading, the woman is praised because she "fears the Lord." Yet in the gospel reading the third servant is condemned because of what his fear compels him to do. What accounts for the difference between these two cases? What is a good way to enact our fear of the Lord? What ways are not so good?

•What valuable gifts has God entrusted to you? Make a list of at least ten things. Which gifts have you multiplied? How have you multiplied these gifts? What good have you accomplished with them? What can you do to act more faithfully with God's gifts?

# CHRIST THE KING

## Staying in the kingdom

*[November 24, 1996; November 21, 1999; November 24, 2002]*

### First Reading: Ezekiel 34:11–12, 15–17

*I myself will look after and tend my sheep.*

Ezekiel's chapter 34 explores images of the people of Israel as sheep, and of the various shepherds who have tended the chosen people. These verses hint at the chapter's riches.

Speaking for God the prophet utters, "I will tend my sheep, as any shepherd must do when they are scattered. I will rescue them and give them rest, binding the injured and healing the sick, but destroying the sleek and the strong. I will judge between any two sheep, and between rams and goats."

The rest of the chapter describes the bad leaders who have led the people into exile, and the fate of the few who have prospered at the expense of the many under those leaders. It also promises a restored covenant between God and the suffering remnant.

### Reponsorial Psalm: Psalm 23:1–2, 2–3, 5–6

### Second Reading: 1 Corinthians 15:20–26, 28

*...in Christ all will come to life again....*

The epistle describes the end of the world. The end has begun. Christ has been raised from the dead, the first fruits of those who sleep. When he returns, all who belong to him will be raised. After destroying all earthly powers, Christ will hand over the kingdom to the Father.

We cannot disregard these words without also doing some harm to our faith. After all, Paul's thought has virtually given shape to three of our four Gospel accounts. Still, we must not worry ourselves about the end, as some do, for such a misplaced emphasis could also distort our faith. Our world will end, there will be a final judgment. Christ will welcome his elect.

The accounts of the gospel that are included in our Bible are much newer than the Pauline epistles. Each evangelist has created a narrative influenced by Paul and other early Christian theologians, as well as by various traditions about Jesus and the specific needs of a local church. Paul's theology pervades the accounts of Matthew, Mark, and Luke. The kingdom parables in these gospels are built upon the foundation illuminated in this epistle text. We must interpret everything through the pivotal event in history—Christ's Easter—for it is here that history's final chapter begins.

## Gospel: Matthew 25:31–46
*...as often as you did it for the least, you did it for me.*

According to Matthew, this is Jesus' concluding and climactic teaching. It describes the final judgment. The Son of Man will separate all the nations into two groups, as a shepherd separates sheep from goats. He will give the sheep the kingdom prepared for them. They will dwell in the kingdom because when he was hungry they fed him, when he was naked they clothed him, when he was ill they comforted him, and when he was imprisoned they visited him. They have done all these things whenever they fed, clothed, comforted, and visited "the least" of humanity. The goats will not fare so well. They have seen and ignored Christ's hunger, nakedness, illness, and imprisonment, whenever they have turned their back on fellow human beings.

The gospel's social teaching could hardly be more explicit or urgent. Matthew climaxes all of Jesus' teaching about the kingdom with a simple and challenging principle: What you do to the least of humanity, you do to me. Like the parables of the dragnet (Matthew 13:47–50, 17th Sunday in ordinary time, year A) and the bridesmaids (Matthew 25:1–13, 32nd Sunday in ordinary time, year A), this teaching describes a gathering. Everyone is invited to the kingdom, and up to a point everyone is included. But, in the end, only those who have conducted themselves appropriately will inherit the kingdom. Only those who have fed, clothed, comforted, and visited will earn a place. This teaching leaves no room for self-righteousness or indifference to the plight of others. It insists that we meet Christ in all other people, and it holds us to account for the ways in which we act.

## Questions for Reflection

• According to the first reading's terms, what sort of sheep are you? If you are lost, wounded, or ill, how did you get that way? Or how did you become sleek and strong?

• How often do you think about judgment day? How important a role does it play in your conduct of your day-to-day affairs?

• Who is hungry? Who is thirsty, naked, lonely, ill, or in prison? What are you doing to help these people?

# ASSUMPTION
## AUGUST 15
### *Power and glory*
*[Replaces 20th Sunday in ordinary time, 1999]*

The Assumption is a doctrinal feast, like the solemnities of the Trinity and Corpus Christi. It celebrates an aspect of Catholic belief that has been revealed to the church at a time in history somewhat later than the creation of the most recently written words in the Bible. On this feast we celebrate the teaching that Mary was assumed directly into heaven.

### First Reading: Revelation 11:19; 12:1–6, 10
*Now have salvation and power come.*

It is a mistake to read the book of Revelation, also known as the Apocalypse, as a book of prediction, although many people today do just that. Its visions of dragons and armies and cosmic battles are actually complex interpretations of history and belief.

A woman clothed in sun and stars wails as she labors to give birth. A dragon destroys vast portions of the sky as it approaches her, and stands before her ready to devour the child. But when the child appears he is taken to God's throne. The woman flees to the desert, and after a battle in which the dragon is destroyed, a voice booms from heaven, proclaiming, "Now have salvation and power come." In the face of terrifying images of power, the baby triumphs. Christ has turned all of our notions of power upside down.

### Responsorial Psalm: Psalm 45:10, 11, 12, 16

### Second Reading: 1 Corinthians 15:20–26
*Christ must reign....*

Paul draws a parallel between Adam and Christ. The one has brought death into the world, while the other brings life. Christ is the first fruits of those who have fallen asleep. He also draws a structured and certain picture of the final judgment. At Christ's coming, all who belong to him will live anew. After destroying all earthly powers, Christ will hand over the kingdom to the Father.

Catholics might not like this kind of talk, because of what some other Christians do with it. Some people twist this and similar texts into assumptions about "rapture" and a self-righteousness that does not seem Christian. These rules are built upon a narrow and misleading interpretation of selected biblical texts.

The central mistake in this kind of thinking is the role of Christ's second coming. Some people focus upon it so much that they act as though the first coming never happened. They may protest that Easter is very important to them, but their fascination with the end clearly overwhelms everything else. An authentic Christian life recognizes Easter as the turning point of all history. We must interpret everything through this pivotal event, for it is here that history's final chapter has already begun. Easter has offered salvation to all of us, while holding us responsible to one another. We prepare for the final judgment by taking up our crosses and by following Christ's example, not by following someone's idea of rules anticipating the end.

### Gospel: Luke 1:39–56
*My being proclaims the greatness of the Lord.*
This text illustrates Mary's special blessedness. Having learned that she bears God's child, Mary races through the hill country to visit Elizabeth. Filled with the Holy Spirit, Elizabeth recognizes the child in Mary's womb: "Blessed is she who trusted that the Lord's words to her would be fulfilled." And Mary responds with what we now call the *Magnificat*. Rich with allusions to the Jewish Bible, this poem consists of two parts framed by an introduction and a conclusion. In the first part Mary sings in gratitude to the Holy One who has done great things for her. In the second part she cites examples of God's actions on behalf of Israel, elevating the humble and bringing down the mighty. The two parts reinforce and interpret one another. God acts on behalf of the powerless, turning conventional expectations upside down.

### Questions for Reflection
•How would you depict a battle for the earth and all its people? What images would you use? What images enact this struggle in much of the book of Revelation? Why are a woman and child introduced into battle? In what ways are the woman and child even more powerful than dragons and armies? Why are they more powerful?

•How do you prepare for the judgment to come? How often do you think about it? How big a role does it play in your everyday conduct?

•How does Mary's example inspire or challenge you?

•How does God act on behalf of the world's lowly? Through whom does God act?

# ALL SAINTS
## NOVEMBER 1
*An invitation for everybody*

### First Reading: Revelation 7:2–4, 9–14
*There was a huge crowd which no one could count.*

This text might make us uncomfortable. After all, is it couched in visions, and such things are scarcely credible in our skeptical century. Even worse, it seems to portray not only the end of a human life but the end of all human life. Worse yet, it insists that there is to be a judgment exercised on the basis of each person's performance in "the trial" (verse 14). Many people today resist the notion of our lives on earth as any form of trial. But as we react to some things that we might not like, let us not lose sight of the profound hopefulness carried through this text. There is room for everyone in God's kingdom.

Having seen several visions, John now looks upon a crowd so vast that no one could count it. The people who make up this crowd have joined with angels and otherworldly creatures to cry out, "Salvation is from our God...and from the Lamb!"

Who are all these people? They are the ones who have washed their robes in the blood of the Lamb. But who are they? They are people from every time and place in history, from every walk of life and from the whole range of races and family and circumstances. They are tall and short, young and old, chubby and slender, and everything in between. What do these people have in common? There are two things: their humanity and their single-hearted commitment to God's will.

### Responsorial Psalm: Psalm 24:1–2, 3–4, 5–6

### Second Reading: 1 John 3:1–3
*Dearly beloved, we are God's children now.*

The writer reminds us who we really are, and how we got to be who we are. God's love, not our actions, has made us children of God. What this means is not yet clear, but eventually God's children will see God and become just like God. Our choices and actions remain important. We must always wait in hope for what is most true to our nature.

## Gospel: Matthew 5:1–12

*Blest are the single-hearted.*

There is room for everyone in God's kingdom. Imagine a scene on a hillside in ancient Palestine. You are surrounded by people, more people than you can count, and, like everyone else, you gaze toward the top of the hill. Jesus begins to speak, and you strain to listen. The crowd quiets down, and you hear, "If you know sorrow or hunger or thirst, if you desire peace or holiness or some connection with God, the kingdom of God is yours."

There is room for everyone in the list that we know as the beatitudes. We have all known sorrow and pain, and need and want. We know what it is to fall short of our goals, to fail, to stand by watching others succeed. In these very familiar verses Jesus pronounces "Blessed" the entire range of human experience. He has made holy the deepest recesses of our hearts, minds, and souls. Matthew tells us that Jesus blesses us all at the beginning of his teaching career, offering the kingdom to everyone.

What does it take to stay in the kingdom? Jesus offers a clue in the beatitudes: We must live in hope. The rest of the sermon on the mount (Matthew 5–7) expounds on this clue, and the remainder of Matthew's gospel portrays Jesus living the kingdom before our eyes.

The feast of All Saints may be our most "catholic" feast. It is "for everybody." Today we remember and celebrate the saints who have gone before us, but we also celebrate what is most true to our human nature. We are God's children. We are invited to discover what it is to be God's children, by living a single-hearted commitment to God's will.

## Questions for Reflection

•In what ways is your life too complicated? What must you do to simplify matters?

•How are you poor in spirit? How and when do you fall short of your hopes, your dreams, your potential?

•What difference does it make that you are one of God's children? How does God's gift to you also place obligations on you?

# IMMACULATE CONCEPTION
## DECEMBER 8
### *God's promise and our response*

A doctrinal feast, the Immaculate Conception celebrates Mary's first moment of existence, in the womb of her mother, St. Ann. Many people assume mistakenly that the feast commemorates Mary's conception of Jesus. Rather, it celebrates an event which occurred a full generation before his birth—the beginning of his mother's life. Together with the Assumption (August 15), the solemnity of the Immaculate Conception honors Mary's life as something extraordinary and worth imitating, from beginning to end. Conceived without sin, Mary is the model Christian who has accepted God's will and shown us how to do the same.

### First Reading: Genesis 3:9–15, 20
*Why did you do such a thing?*

There are probably more differing ways to read the creation stories in Genesis than any other portion of the Bible. These particular verses from the second creation story seem to favor an understanding of original sin. The man has eaten the forbidden fruit from the tree of knowledge of good and evil, and of everything in between. The man appears to have caved in to the temptation to seek to know everything, to become like God, or at least "like a god." When God, brokenhearted, confronts the man and the woman, they make matters worse. The man blames the woman for his action, while she blames the serpent. If the first sin is a pride that can lead to idolatry, then the second sin is a refusal to take responsibility. The two sins stand together to portray the role of evil in the human condition. We demand to be our own gods, but we are also eager to blame the nearest scapegoat for the consequences. Given this sorry state of affairs, maybe it is a miracle that God has commuted the sentence to hard labor. In the end, the man and the woman venture out from the garden that was once their home, to make their living on the land. To be human is to work hard, to seek companionship, and to cope with our ever-present capacity to sin. It is also to seek God among the various things of our lives.

**Responsorial Psalm: Psalm 98:1, 2–3, 3–4**

**Second Reading: Ephesians 1:3–6, 11–12**

*God chose us in him....*

One of the sources of the Calvinist doctrine of predestination appears in this text. The author, probably a disciple of Paul, teaches Gentile Christians at Ephesus, the site of the cult of the goddess Artemis/ Diana. They are to be God's adopted children, because God has chosen them before the world began. Having once been pagans, these people are now adopted children.

**Gospel: Luke 1:26–38**

*Blessed are you among women.*

It is easy to see why many people are confused about the focus of this feast. This text describes the angel's announcement to Mary that she will bear a son, who will be called the Son of the Most High. Even so, the feast celebrates Mary, her purity, and above all, her faithful response to everything that has been proposed to her.

Mary shows us a right way to walk before God. Her actions contrast greatly with those of the first man and woman. If ever a promise is tough to swallow, Gabriel's words to Mary surely demand faith. This story embraces many themes. One involves Jewish hopes for a Messiah, which are, according to Christians, fulfilled in the baby. Another speaks of the power of God, in whose hands the laws of nature are simply the tools of creation. What may be the most important theme is that the faith of a frightened young girl bears earth-shaking consequences.

This feast celebrates that human person who, unique among all of us, was favored to carry God inside her body. More important, it also invites all of us to walk rightly before God, as she has done.

## Questions for Reflection

•How would you like to be "like a god"? What would you gain? What would you lose, if anything? How do you deal with this most powerful temptation from day to day? What resources do you need to help you face this temptation?

•What has God promised to you? Which of God's promises are more difficult to swallow than others? What do you have to do in order to cooperate with God's promises?

•What lessons does Mary offer to you? How does her example inspire or challenge you?

# APPENDIX

# DIVING DEEPER—AN INVITATION TO A GOOD CONVERSATION

Let us suppose you accept this book's invitation to explore the word of the Lord. You quickly grow dissatisfied with swimming on the surface of biblical texts. Whether or not you like or agree with my explanations of the readings, you recognize that they introduce you to a world that you want to explore in depth.

What do you do? There are many possibilities: You could attend lectures and workshops, or you could take classes at a local college or university. You might drive yourself, page-by-page, through a scholarly commentary. You might take a correspondence course. You might participate in a forum conducted via computer and modem on an online bulletin board.

Whatever you choose, I encourage you to participate in some form of genuine *conversation* with biblical texts. Let me explain what I mean. I first encountered this way of thinking about biblical interpretation in Bernard Lee's article "Shared Homily: Conversation that Puts Communities At Risk." Distilling the important and difficult work of thinkers like Hans-Georg Gadamer, Paul Ricoeur, Bernard Lonergan, and David Tracy, Lee advocates a simple procedure. This procedure acknowledges and deals with the complications that must arise when relentlessly meaning-making people approach a text from their unique perspectives. It is the best way I know to make honest interpretations.

Lee's procedure consists of three stages. In a first stage, reading alone, or better, with a group, you declare initial responses to a text. These usually include likes and dislikes, questions and insights, as well as other things. When all the initial responses have been declared, you proceed to a second stage, in which you consider various scholarly commentaries. It is healthy if you can find honest disagreement among scholars. What you are after in this stage is what

Lee and others speak of as the "horizon" of the text. Here you are asking questions about the author's historical circumstances, worldview, and intent, about literary devices and textual variants that affect the shape of the text, about the various ways in which the text has already been interpreted, and more.

Having examined the text's horizon in greater or lesser detail, you then proceed to a third phase in which you determine what the text means. You do this by identifying correlations, or intersections, between the text's horizon and your initial impressions. There are three possible kinds of correlations. First, your initial impressions might coincide exactly with the text's horizon. In other words, it nestles comfortably inside the horizon. Because the worlds portrayed in the Bible differ so much from our own, however, it is more likely that your initial impression will collide with the text's horizon, that it will not fit. In this instance, you face a choice. A second possible correlation, then, is that you collide with the text and that you choose not to change your mind. There is a disagreement between what you see in the text and in the text's horizon, and you choose to live with this disagreement. You agree to disagree. The third possibility is that you collide with the text but that you accept its challenge. You decide to try to enter into and live in the text's horizon. Clearly, this latter decision is a step in a person's continuing conversion. Maybe you can begin to see why the lectionary is a uniquely powerful instrument for celebrating conversion in the ongoing life of the church, and particularly in the catechumenate.

Notice the role of *voices* in this procedure. In the first stage, you hear your own voice, and the voices of any other people who share with you the task of interpreting. But you do not allow any of these voices to become "the meaning" of the text. At this point you still have a long way to go. You exercise restraint to defer any judgments about meaning until after you have enlarged the conversation. In the second stage, you listen to voices of others who wear the mantles of "expert." Finally, now that you have listened, you can make informed judgments about the meaning or meanings of a text. (A single text may sometimes support more than one meaning.)

A good conversation includes a wide variety of voices. All participants listen. They really listen. An interpretation that emerges from a conversation that includes a wide variety of voices is sure to be more adequate than one that comes from a single voice or a narrow band of voices.

Am I suggesting that we determine meaning by majority vote? Wouldn't a procedure like this leave us at the mercy of a loud crackpot or a forceful-if-misguided written commentary? No, I do not advocate either majority rule or a tyranny of the loudest voice. In fact, I am calling for the opposite of the latter. With Bernard Lee and others, I insist that we take care not to exclude differing voices in our conversation. To make sure that all voices contribute to a real conversation, let me suggest these rules, formulated by David Tracy:

- Say only what you mean;
- Say it as accurately as you can;
- Listen to and respect what the other says, however difficult;
- Be willing to correct or defend your opinions if challenged;
- Be willing to argue if necessary, confront if demanded, endure necessary conflict, change your mind if the evidence suggests.

I hope you will keep these thoughts in mind as you look for a way to go more deeply into biblical texts. Listen for a variety of voices in a conversation in which all can be heard with respect. Also, perhaps now you can appreciate why Bernard Lee speaks of "risk" in the title of his article. A genuine conversation is risky. It might require that we change. A conversation with biblical texts places many of our assumptions and habits at risk. But as millions have known, the risks are worthwhile.

Since I do invite you into conversation with texts, I cannot recommend most of what is called "Bible study," as it is manifested in various churches. Too often, such programs offer only a very narrow band of voices or a single voice. They make the mistake of substituting someone's first impressions for a genuine interpretation of a text. Invariably, this is a prescription for mischief.

Ironically, this kind narrowness may occur more often in "non-denominational fellowships" than anywhere else. Here is an example of what I mean: At the invitation of a friend, recently I attended the "newcomers night" hosted by the local chapter of a nationally-known Bible study program. The welcome seemed genuine enough, but the orientation for newcomers struck me as overly burdened with program rules and demands. Now, I do not object to discipline, especially if it seems worthwhile, but on this occasion I grew increasingly uneasy with what seemed to be a literalist and authoritarian approach to the Bible. My unease went crazy during an hour-long lecture about the day's text, which confirmed all my suspicions about the program. It is literalist and authoritarian. Worse, it rejects biblical scholarship. It does not admit ordained ministers into its "fellowship," ostensibly to maintain lay control. In practice, however, this refusal to admit ministers virtually guarantees that the program will continue to be dominated by a single voice, that of a lay preacher who relies upon the program's approved sources, and who refuses to hear voices that might disturb what he happens to find in the Bible.

Do not misunderstand me. I am not condemning everything that goes by the name "Bible study." I do want to illustrate my discomfort with some manifestations of that term that are all too common. I also want to urge you to be careful. The criteria of good conversation should help you in this regard. I am suspicious of anything that does not place you in regular conversation with many different voices surrounding a biblical text. I hope you will exercise a similar suspicion.

For a more in-depth appreciation of what I call "conversation," please consult the following sources:

Dunning, James B. (1993) *Echoing God's Word.* Arlington, VA: The North American Forum on the Catechumenate.

Lee, Bernard (1987) "Shared Homily: Conversation that Puts Communities at Risk." *Alternative Futures for Worship, volume 3: The Eucharist.* Collegeville, MN: Liturgical Press, pp. 157-174.

McBrien, Philip J. (1992) *How to Teach with the Lectionary.* Mystic, CT: Twenty-Third Publications.

McBrien, Philip J. (1992) *How to Teach with the Lectionary: Leader's Guide.* Mystic, CT: Twenty-Third Publications.

Tracy, David (1984) Chapters 16-18 in R. Grant with D. Tracy *A Short History of the Interpretation of the Bible* (2d ed., rev. and enlarged). Philadelphia: Fortress.

Tracy, David (1987) *Plurality and Ambiguity.* San Francisco: Harper & Row.

# Of Related Interest...

### Bringing the Word to Life, Year A
*Scripture Messages That Change Lives*
Michael R. Kent
The readings for every Sunday of the year are covered, with the
two-page reflections serving as the foundation for ongoing
translation of Scripture to daily life.

ISBN: 0-89622-639-5, 160 pp, $9.95

### Scripture Reflections Day by Day
Rev. Joseph Donders
These Gospel meditations—366 in all—are current, timely, short
enough to be read in any free moment and full of meaning and
hope.

ISBN: 0-89622-494-5, 384 pp, $9.95

### Lightly Goes the Good News
*Making the Gospel Your Own Story*
Andre Papineau
This book offers unique and light-hearted insights into the
characters and stories of the New Testament..

ISBN: 0-89622-376-0, 144 pp, $7.95

### Seek Treasures in Small Fields
*Everyday Holiness*
Joan Puls
Puls encourages readers to tap into the "treasures" that lie
beneath the "small fields" of everyday life circumstances.

ISBN: 0-89622-509-7, 160 pp, $7.95

*Available at religious bookstores or from*
**TWENTY-THIRD PUBLICATIONS**
P.O. Box 180 • Mystic, CT 06355

1-800-321-0411